The Broken Sword of Justice is a concise, coherent account of the tragic events in the Middle East over the past sixty years. It is also a powerful and well-documented indictment of America's role in those events.

Margaret Arakie has had a long and varied career with the United Nations. After working for the League of Nations, she went to New York in 1946 on the staff of the U.N. A year later she was appointed Assistant Secretary to the U.N. Special Committee on Palestine and went to the Middle East. She was on the staff of the U.N. Mediator for Palestine, Count Folke Bernadotte, and was later political officer on the U.N. Conciliation Committee for Palestine. Between 1955 and 1967, she worked on the U.N. Relief and Works Agency for Palestinian refugees in Beirut, eventually becoming Special Assistant to U.N.R.W.A.'s Commissioner-General.

THE BROKEN SWORD
OF JUSTICE

America, Israel
and the Palestine tragedy

Ω————————————————————

MARGARET ARAKIE

QUARTET BOOKS   LONDON

First published in Great Britain by Quartet Books Limited 1973
27 Goodge Street, London W1P 1FD

Copyright © 1973 by Margaret Arakie

ISBN 0 704 32022 3 *Casebound edition*
     0 704 33017 2 *Midway edition*

Printed in Great Britain by
Cox & Wyman Ltd, London, Fakenham and Reading

For Elizabeth

ACKNOWLEDGMENTS

My first debt is to my fellow-workers in the United Nations Relief and Works Agency for Palestine Refugees; some ninety-nine per cent are themselves refugees from Palestine. I am also deeply indebted to the authors of many books, only a few of which are listed in my short bibliography. I am grateful for the courteous assistance given me by the Librarians of the Middle East Institute, Washington, D.C., of the London Library, of the United Nations Library in Geneva and the United Nations Information Centre in London; and for invaluable help by the staffs of the Council for the Advancement of Arab-British Understanding and of American Near East Refugee Aid, and by individual experts of many nationalities. My special thanks are due to Dr John H. Davis, President of A.N.E.R.A. and formerly Commissioner-General of U.N.R.W.A., staunch champion in the United States of the rights of the Palestine Arabs, whose generously given advice and encouragement largely made the writing of this book possible.

M.A.

'I do not deny that it is an adventure. Are we never to have adventures? Are we never to try new experiments?' – Lord Balfour, addressing the House of Lords on the question of Britain's acceptance of the mandate for Palestine, June 1922

1. BACKGROUND TO AMERICAN POLICY

When, in November 1917, the thirty-one-year-old David Ben Gurion learned in New York of the Balfour Declaration, he exclaimed:

Britain has made a magnificent gesture. She has recognized our existence as a nation and has acknowledged our right to the country.

The world is still struggling with the legacy of that gesture. It took the form of a letter, sent on 2 November 1917 by Arthur James Balfour, then Britain's Foreign Minister, to Lord Rothschild. It read as follows:

My dear Lord Rothschild,
I have much pleasure in conveying to you, on behalf of His Majesty's Government, the following declaration of sympathy with Jewish Zionist aspirations which has been submitted to, and approved by, the Cabinet.

'His Majesty's Government view with favour the establishment in Palestine of a national home for the Jewish people, and will use their best endeavours to facilitate the achievement of this object, it being clearly understood that nothing shall be done which may prejudice the civil and religious rights of existing non-Jewish communities in Palestine, or the rights and political status enjoyed by Jews in any other country.'

I should be grateful if you would bring this declaration to the knowledge of the Zionist Federation.

Yours
(signed)
A. W. James Balfour

Shortly after the entry of the United States into the First World War in April 1917, the British Foreign Secretary had paid his first visit to America. So far as is known, his discussions with President Wilson did not touch on the general question of Zionism, or on the terms of a possible British declaration of sympathy with Zionist aims. Through Justice Brandeis, a leading American Zionist and a close friend of Wilson's, Balfour was, however, assured of the President's approval for such a move. Subsequently the British government inquired, through Colonel House, Wilson's adviser, whether the President would be willing to issue a public statement endorsing the Balfour Declaration (which was still in draft form). After some weeks of delay, Wilson told House that 'he concurred with the formula suggested from the other side'; but by the time word of this reached London, the draft had been basically revised by the British Cabinet. Wilson did not publicly express approval of the final text of the Balfour Declaration until August 1918, when he sent a message of greeting to American Jews on the occasion of a Jewish New Year meeting in Carnegie Hall, New York. The Secretary of State, Robert Lansing, had earlier advised against the sending of such a message, pointing out that the United States was not at war with Turkey, that the Jews themselves were divided over Zionism and that many Christians would resent the handing over of the Holy Land to the Jews.

Up to the First World War, America's chief concern in the Middle East had, in fact, been the interests of her missionaries and educationists in the territories under Ottoman rule. As many as 150 American-sponsored schools and colleges were established in Syria and Lebanon, the most important being the Syrian Protestant College in Beirut (known after 1919 as the American University of Beirut). The influence of the college on the early stages of the Arab nationalist revival and the impetus it gave to that movement were of great significance.

Some students of history maintain that the United States began to play a part in the Palestine question through her very entry into the First World War. True, she did not bother to declare war on Turkey and thus took no part in the negotiations on, or signature of, the 1920 Treaty of Sèvres, which was concerned with the disposition of the Ottoman Empire's non-Turkish territories, nor in those regarding the Treaty of Lausanne, which superseded the Treaty of Sèvres in 1923. But the prestige of the United States and the fame of President Wilson's doctrine of the self-determination of peoples were such that any idea of an outright annexation of former Ottoman possessions, such as had been envisaged in some of the secret treaties negotiated by the Allies, no longer had much validity. The Arab nationalists naturally attached special importance to the twelfth of Wilson's Fourteen Points, which stated that 'The other nationalities which are now under Turkish rule should be assured an undoubted security of life and an absolutely unmolested opportunity of autonomous development.' At the same time, the Zionists managed to see this statement as signifying the sympathy of the United States government towards Zionism.

For the next two decades, American policy was to be based on benevolent, but essentially detached and passive, approval of the aims of the Balfour Declaration.

Misunderstanding has persisted about Balfour's personal responsibility for the declaration, and some Zionists at the time preferred to refer to it as 'the British Declaration'. In fact, it was a document over which the Imperial War Cabinet had wrestled for three months before the text was ready for issue. This is not to say that Balfour's deep Zionist sympathies had not played a major part in the effort and had not influenced his colleagues, particularly the British Prime Minister, David Lloyd George. Balfour had for long been interested in the Jewish question and had felt strongly about the way in which the Jewish contribution to culture and to religion had for the most part been requited by the Christian world. He had been an enthusiastic supporter of the previous British offer to the Zionists of land in Uganda which was eventually rejected by the Seventh World Zionist Congress in 1905. Subsequently, conversations with Chaim Weizmann, who not long after was to become leader and spokesman of the British Zionists, had convinced Balfour that 'history could not thus be ignored'; if a home was to be found for the Jewish people, it was vain to seek it anywhere but in Palestine. His niece and biographer, Mrs Dugdale, records that, towards the end of his illustrious life, what he had been able to do for the Jews seemed to him on the whole his most worth-while achievement.

Besides Balfour and Lloyd George, the British Cabinet included other convinced Zionists, among them General Smuts and Lord Milner, Secretary of State for War. But it also contained a formidable opponent of Zionism in Lord Curzon as well as in the only Jewish Cabinet member, Edwin Montague, who was concerned in his capacity as Secretary of State for India with the views of the ninety million Moslems in that country, and spokesman of the bitter hostility to Zionism felt at the time by nearly all wealthy and influential British Jews. Their fear was that antisemitism would become rampant everywhere if the Jews allowed themselves to plan for a country of their own or a national political existence outside their present citizenship.

But to what had the United States actually committed itself in endorsing, through President Wilson, the Balfour Declaration? What did the declaration actually mean? Some of its authors would have been profoundly dismayed by Ben Gurion's forthright assumption that it meant nothing less than Jewish statehood. It is now known that the phrase 'the establishment in Palestine of a national home' represented a compromise between the views of those British Cabinet

4

members who were ready to contemplate the ultimate possibility of a Jewish state and those who most decidedly were not. Even among the pro-Zionists, there were variations of interpretation. For his part, Lloyd George – speaking twenty years after the declaration was issued – summed the question up as follows:

> The idea was, and this was the interpretation put upon it at the time, that a Jewish State was not to be set up immediately by the Peace Treaty without reference to the wishes of the majority of the inhabitants. On the other hand, it was contemplated that when the time arrived for according representative institutions to Palestine, if the Jews had meanwhile responded to the opportunity afforded them by the idea of a national home and had become a definite majority of the inhabitants, then Palestine would thus become a Jewish Commonwealth.

As for the motives of the declaration, they were – again according to Lloyd George – of a 'propagandist' nature. In November 1917, the Allied and associated powers faced a critical situation in which it was believed that Jewish sympathy, or the reverse, would make a substantial difference, one way or another, to the Allied cause. Such a view possibly testifies more to the brilliance of Dr Weizmann's persuasive powers than to the perspicacity of the British Prime Minister, for the Zionist movement was still weak, with little influence in Europe or in all-important America. The Zionists were certainly not at that time in a position to give Britain support of any value.

Lloyd George, with his Celtic temperament and biblical scholastic background, was probably more fascinated by the Old Testament overtones of Zionism than concerned with the fate of modern Jewry. The matter was seen in a somewhat different light by Lord Hailey, who was also present during the preparation of the Balfour Declaration. It was, in his view, impossible that the Imperial War Cabinet should have neglected at that time of crisis the rights of Britain's actual allies. The compromise reached, therefore, did not provide merely for the creation of a Jewish home, but also for the safe-guards of the position and rights of the Arabs 'in neither a narrow nor a local sense' – in other words, in a political sense. Although many factors doubtless combined to launch the declaration, it is certain that altruistic, even romantic, sympathy with Zionist hopes was prominent among them.

The Balfour Declaration represented a personal triumph for Chaim Weizmann, the keynote to whose policy had for long been co-operation with Britain and dependence on her for the attainment of the ultimate Zionist goal of a Jewish state. The fortunes of war had placed him in control of the part of the European Zionist Organization which had survived outside the territories of Germany and her allies. Much of the direction of Zionist policy was in his hands, and he was able to steer it towards an initial goal of a Palestine under some form of British protection. The majority of American Zionists, and of those living in other countries, appeared to be content to support this goal. 'We thought,' wrote Nahum Goldmann, 'that we held a promissory note in our hands and we were impatient to see it honoured.'

Unfortunately for Zionism, as Professor Rodinson has pointed out, just at the moment when it decided to direct its efforts towards that goal, 'the natives of that country began to be affected by a similar ideological movement, namely Arab nationalism'.

When the First World War came to an end, most Jews believed that Britain had promised them a Jewish state in Palestine; the Arabs assumed they could count on her support for an independent Arab nation, to include Palestine; and the French were convinced that their claims to Syria had been underwritten.

This appalling tangle was to cause deep and enduring resentment in the Arab world and to prejudice for three decades every attempt at a Palestinian settlement. It came about because, concurrently with their negotiations with the Zionists, the British government had been making promises to the Sherif of Mecca and carrying on secret negotiations with its allies, France and Russia. It is beyond the scope of this

6

book to trace these wartime developments in all their complex detail. In brief, with the objective of enlisting Arab support for the war against Turkey, Sir Henry McMahon, British High Commissioner in Egypt, was authorized in 1915 to promise Sherif Hussein of Mecca British support for Arab independence in certain Arab areas of the Ottoman Empire defined by the Sherif himself, subject to the exclusion of the Syrian coastal region and in so far as the Sherif's territorial claims were not inconsistent with French interests. A key passage in McMahon's letter of 24 October 1915 to Sherif Hussein (which formed part of a lengthy correspondence) states:

> The two districts of Mersina and Alexandretta and portions of Syria lying to the west of the districts of Damascus, Homs, Hama and Aleppo cannot be said to be purely Arab and should be excluded from the proposed limits and boundaries. With the above modification, and without prejudice to our existing treaties with Arab chiefs, we accept these limits and boundaries. . . .

Palestine was regarded by the Arabs as forming part of Syria and many persons engaged in the negotiations, or closely in touch with the problem, later attested that it was the British intention to exclude Palestine from the promised area of independence, and that this had been well understood by the Sherif. But it seems equally apparent, from a reading of the McMahon–Hussein correspondence, that McMahon's letters did not clearly convey British intentions.*

About the same time as these approaches were being made to Sherif Hussein, Anglo-French negotiations were being carried on by M. Georges Picot and Sir Mark Sykes, in consultation with the Russian government. They resulted in May

---

* The confusion arose because of the discrepancy between the Arabic word 'wilaya', a term related to the Turkish 'vilayet' or administrative district, and the use of the English word 'district' as its equivalent. There was no land west of the Vilayet of Aleppo, which extended to the sea, and there were no Vilayets of Homs or Hama. Presumably McMahon used the word 'district' in the sense of 'vicinity' and thus excluded the area roughly northwards from Sidon to Alexandretta, but not Palestine.

1916 in the Sykes–Picot Agreement which, with the post-war settlement in view, divided the Arab area of the Ottoman Empire north of the Arabian Peninsula into zones to be controlled by one or other of the three allies. Palestine was to be 'subjected to a special régime to be determined by agreement between Russia, France and Great Britain'. The agreement was kept secret until 1917, when the Russian Bolshevik government published a copy of it. Thus it was without knowledge of any British commitment other than the McMahon Pledge, and, of course, in total ignorance of the fact that the Zionists had already secured the support of several leading British statesmen for their aims, that the Sherif in June 1916 launched the Arab Revolt against the Turks, his forces operating on the outer flank of the British advance towards Damascus.

On his visit to America in 1917, Balfour felt it his duty to tell President Wilson about the various secret treaties concluded by the Allies, including the Sykes–Picot Agreement; but he received the impression that the President was more interested in the present and the future, and did not attach much importance to these undertakings.

By early November 1917 General Allenby had captured Beersheba and British forces were advancing up the coastal plain of Palestine. On 9 December 1917 they entered Jerusalem. A British military administration was immediately set up in the occupied area, though it did not extend to the whole country until the Turks were finally expelled from all parts of Palestine in the autumn of 1918.

Lloyd George's government was soon informed by its representatives in the Middle East that the Balfour Declaration had come as a severe shock to the Arab world. The government instructed Commander Hogarth, head of their Arab Bureau in Cairo, to explain to King Hussein of the Hedjaz (as the Sherif had become) that a national home for the Jews was, indeed, to be established, but only in so far as it was compatible with the economic and political freedom of the existing population. The British government was determined, the king was assured, that in Palestine 'no people shall be subject to the other'. Years later, the then Colonial Secretary, Malcolm MacDonald, was to tell the Permanent Mandates Commission of the League of Nations that this assurance to the Arabs could only have meant that Palestine 'could not one day become a Jewish State against the will of the Arabs of the country'. Thus the process of whittling down the Balfour Declaration was attempted by the very government which had issued it, and begun only a few weeks after the declaration had been signed.

In the spring of 1919 a curious episode occurred. President Wilson was attending the Paris Peace Conference, where he was the dominant figure. On 4 March, when he was on a brief visit to Washington, the Egyptian press published the following text as an official communiqué from the American Diplomatic Agency in Cairo:

A Jewish Delegation, headed by Judge Julian Mack of Chicago, interviewed the President regarding the future of Palestine. The President expressed his sympathy with the principle of the incontestable right of the Jewish people everywhere to equality of status and recalled that he had previously expressed his personal approval to the British Government of a declaration respecting the historic claims of the Jews regarding Palestine. He said he was persuaded that the Allied Nations, with the fullest concurrence of our own Government and people, are agreed that in Palestine shall be laid the foundations of a Jewish Commonwealth.

Delicate negotiations on the future of the Middle East were taking place in Paris and the communiqué was something of a bombshell. Its authenticity was questioned at one of the daily meetings of the Commissioners Plenipotentiary in Paris, at which the Secretary of State, Lansing, represented the United States.

The Commissioners [the minutes of the meeting record] very much doubted whether the President had ever made such a statement, but requested that it be sent to the President. . . . They desired that the President be asked whether this quotation were correct and that it be added that in case

9

it were not correct, they were of the opinion that it should be denied at once.

On 16 April President Wilson, by then back in Paris, wrote to Lansing:

Of course I did not use any of the words in the enclosed and they do not indeed purport to be my words. But I did in substance say what is quoted, though the expression 'foundation of a Jewish Commonwealth' goes a little further than my idea at the time. All that I meant was to corroborate our expressed acquiescence in the position of the British Government with regard to the future of Palestine.

The President's supposed statement has been quoted time and again, and was even used in the authoritative report of the British Royal Commission on Palestine in 1937 as incontrovertible evidence of how Wilson interpreted the ambiguous term 'National Home'. The American Zionists had indeed scored an invaluable point. Significantly they then, and invariably in the future, referred to the Balfour Declaration as though it had one purpose only and did not form a dual undertaking to Arabs and Jews.

Meanwhile, during those spring months, the American, British, French and Italian government leaders on the Supreme Council of the Peace Conference were at loggerheads over the allocation of the mandate for Syria. In an endeavour to break the deadlock, President Wilson pointed out that the wishes of the population concerned should be the determining element in the choice of a mandatory power. Taking up a suggestion which had been put to the Supreme Council a month earlier by Dr Howard Bliss, President of the Syrian Protestant College in Beirut, Wilson proposed that an international commission should be sent forthwith to the Levant to ascertain local views on the matter. The advisers to the various governments represented at the Peace Conference pointed out that the presence of such a body might add to the existing unrest in Syria; but the international commission's terms of reference, drafted by Wilson, were quickly approved by Clemenceau and Lloyd George and the appointment of the two American members, Henry C. King and Charles R. Crane, followed without loss of time. It soon, however, became obvious that the French government actually intended to take no part in an inquiry which might well result in publicizing anti-French sentiments in Syria. The British, who had also announced their nominees, thereupon withdrew from participation in the commission. President Wilson, however, insisted that his proposal should go ahead, and at the end of May 1919 the two American commissioners left for the Middle East.

They spent forty days in Syria and Palestine and subsequently reported that the Arab Moslems were almost unanimous in wanting an independent, united Syria, that the Arab Christians hoped for an effective mandate, and that the Jews, who – as the commissioners noted – represented only just over one tenth of the population of Palestine, favoured the Zionist programme and British control over the country. The King–Crane Report warned the Peace Conference that anti-Zionist feeling in Palestine and throughout Syria was intense and not lightly to be flouted. They pointed out that 'a National Home for the Jewish people was not the same thing as the transformation of Palestine into a Jewish state; nor could the creation of such a state be brought about without very serious prejudice to the civil and religious rights of existing non-Jewish communities in Palestine'. The report proposed the establishment of a mandate for a limited period for Syria, including Palestine. The state should be a constitutional monarchy under the Emir Feisal and should allow for the autonomy of special areas, such as the Lebanon. As to a mandatory power, the population as a whole favoured the United States, with Britain as second choice. The commissioners recommended that the mandate should under no circumstances be given to France, though if a compromise were necessary, the Lebanon might be detached from Syria and entrusted to a French mandate.

The King–Crane Report was duly filed with the American delegation to the Peace Conference, but it was not made public. Neither the United States nor Britain was prepared to accept a mandate for Syria and nothing would induce the

French to give up their claims. The report was ignominiously shelved. But although it officially remained a dead letter, it was, in the view of some experts, not without influence in strengthening the British government's subsequent tendency to restrict and moderate Zionist aspirations.

In April 1920, the principal Allied Powers, meeting in San Remo, decided that Britain should be entrusted with the mandate for Palestine, adding that the mandatory power was to be responsible for giving effect to the Balfour Declaration. A civil administration, with as High Commissioner Sir Herbert Samuel, for long a supporter of Zionism, replaced the military rule on 1 July 1920. The mandate itself was finally approved by the Council of the League of Nations in July 1922 and entered into force on 29 September 1923. In addition to reproducing the text of the Balfour Declaration in its preamble, the mandate recognized 'the historical connection of the Jewish people with Palestine' and the grounds for reconstituting their national home in that country (a phrase the Zionists had tried in vain to introduce into the Declaration). Further, it commanded the mandatory power to secure the establishment of the National Home, to co-operate with 'an appropriate Jewish Agency', which was to assist and take part in the development of the country; and to facilitate Jewish immigration and encourage close settlement of Jews on the land. The mandate thus brought the realization of Zionist dreams substantially nearer to the plane of seemingly practical possibilities, and secured for the Jews the triumph of international ratification of their aims.

But long before the mandate had entered officially into force, the impossibility of fulfilling the wishes of both Arabs and Jews had become clear. Arab riots broke out in northern Palestine in March 1920, and, more severely, in Jerusalem a few weeks later. Further anti-Jewish outbreaks followed in 1921. A Palestine Arab delegation declared in London in 1922 that the Arabs of the country could accept 'no constitution which would fall short of giving the peoples of Palestine full control of their own affairs'. If they acknowledged the legality of the mandate and the Jewish National Home, the statement continued, the Arabs 'would be in the position of agreeing to an instrument of government which might, and probably would, be used to smother their national life under a flood of alien immigration'. In the House of Lords, a Liberal peer, Lord Islington, introduced a successful motion stating that the mandate was unacceptable, 'because it directly violates the pledges made by His Majesty's Government to the people of Palestine . . . and is, as at present framed, opposed to the sentiments and wishes of the great majority of those people'.

The widespread unrest in Palestine and the mounting opposition at home forced the British to issue a commentary on the mandate, which was published in July 1922 and became known as the Churchill White Paper (Winston Churchill being at the time the Minister responsible for the Colonial Office, the department which issued the document). The British government, the 1922 White Paper explained, had at no time envisaged 'the disappearance or subordination of the Arabic population, language or culture in Palestine'. The Balfour Declaration, it contended, did not contemplate that Palestine as a whole should be converted into a Jewish National Home, but that such a home should be founded in Palestine.

When it is asked what is meant by the development of a Jewish National Home in Palestine, it may be answered that it is not the imposition of a Jewish nationality upon the inhabitants of Palestine as a whole, but the further development of the existing Jewish community . . . in order that it may become a centre in which the Jewish people as a whole may take, on grounds of religion and race, an interest and a pride.

The Zionist reaction was predictably unenthusiastic. The Arabs of Palestine rejected the Churchill memorandum altogether. But the League of Nations confirmed the mandate on the basis of the interpretation given it by this British statement of policy.

Two months later, in Washington, President Warren G. Harding affixed his signature to a joint resolution which had been adopted, as a result of energetic Zionist lobbying, by both Houses of Congress on 30 June of that year, and which read:

> Resolved by the Senate and the House of Representatives of the United States in Congress assembled, that the United States of America favors the establishment in Palestine of a National Home for the Jewish people, it being clearly understood that nothing shall be done which may prejudice the civil and religious rights of Christian and all other non-Jewish communities in Palestine, and that the Holy Places and religious buildings and sites in Palestine shall be adequately protected.

However, the House Committee on Foreign Affairs, conforming to the prevalent isolationist mood of the country, pointed out that the resolution merely expressed 'our moral interest ... [and] commits us to no foreign obligations or entanglements'. A see-saw pattern had emerged, whereby the official, basically neutral American policy was periodically interrupted by expressions of sympathy – almost always for Zionist goals and as a result of vigorous Zionist pressures – by presidents, statesmen or by the Congress.

For nearly twenty-four years, American relations with Palestine had as their formal basis the Anglo-American Convention of 1924, in which the United States government, as a non-member of the League of Nations, approved the mandate for Palestine and the choice of Britain as mandatory power. The preamble to the convention recited – at the request of the British government – the full text of the mandate (a fact which later prompted various parties to claim that the United States had the right to have a say in any changes to the mandate); but the substantive articles were concerned to ensure that American nationals should enjoy 'all the rights and benefits secured under the terms of the mandate to nationals of League members'. The convention, and similiar instruments relating to the other Middle East mandates, in fact came about as a result of pressures by American business firms for equal commercial opportunities in mandated territories in the

14

Middle East. The government had already been able to secure for a group of American oil companies a 23.75 per cent share in the Iraq Petroleum Company and had been endeavouring to obtain from the two mandatory powers concerned – France and Britain – general commitments to an open-door policy which would not discriminate against American business interests. These conventions later enabled American oil interests to consolidate and dramatically expand their foothold in the region.

From 1922 onwards, the British veered first in one direction and then in another, in a desperate effort to reconcile their own contradictory promises and the inherent contradiction of the terms of the mandate. The Arabs found they were able to obtain concessions by resorting to violence; the Jews discovered they could influence decisions in their favour by appealing to the parliamentary parties and to British public opinion. Successive commissions of inquiry arrived in Palestine from London and unvaryingly reported that the underlying cause of trouble was Arab resentment at Jewish attempts to take over their country.

Violence rose and fell in direct ratio to the size of the Jewish population. In the two relatively peaceful years beginning in January 1926, for example, only 15,794 Jews entered the country and as many as 12,023 emigrated from it. But in 1929 an incident at the Wailing Wall in Jerusalem resulted in bloodshed in the Holy City and further afield. Two commissions of inquiry followed each other in rapid succession. Simultaneously with the second of the two reports, the traditionally pro-Zionist Labour government in Britain published a White Paper signed by Lord Passfield (Sidney Webb), Secretary of State for the Colonies, which declared flatly that there was no land available for further Jewish agricultural settlement; that a more stringent immigration policy was necessary; and that a scheme was to be introduced to ensure the rights of Arab tenants to subsistence plots. Finally, it announced that the British government held that the obligations laid down in the mandate in regard to the two sections of the population were of equal weight.

Thereupon a storm of totally unexpected violence broke over the heads of the unfortunate Labour Ministers. Weizmann described the Passfield memorandum as a curtailment of the progress of the National Home and prepared a letter of resignation from the presidency of the Zionist Organization and the Jewish Agency; Lord Melchett, in a public letter resigning from the Council of the Jewish Agency, branded the Passfield statement as 'a grotesque travesty of the purpose of the mandate'; three Conservative leaders in an open letter accused the government of issuing a statement contrary to the spirit of the Balfour Declaration and of every British announcement of policy on Palestine for the last twelve years; Lloyd George demanded that Britain either implement or surrender the mandate; and from South Africa, General Smuts cabled to the Prime Minister, Ramsay MacDonald, urging the immediate repudiation of the White Paper. Official Washington, however, remained calm and did not admit of any latitude in the interpretation of the Anglo-American Convention. When a Zionist delegation appealed for government intervention, the brisk response of Stimson, the Secretary of State, was that his duty was to protect United States citizens, not the Zionist movement.

The British government, in their alarm at the anger of the Jews and its political repercussions, shifted their policy in dizzying fashion. No sooner had the protests commenced, than they began to try to explain away their own policy; and on 13 February 1931 Ramsay MacDonald read out in the House of Commons a letter to Weizmann purporting to clarify the Passfield paper, but in effect interpreting it in a spirit contrary to its original drafting. Though many Zionists were dissatisfied because the letter was not an outright repudiation of the 'Black Paper', as they called it, the Zionist Organization received it as an acceptable recognition of Jewish rights under the mandate. The Arabs, however, were indignant that their expected victory had been snatched away from them by what they naturally saw as a cynical reversal of government policy brought about by the political power of Zionism. Britain's uncertain efforts to be simultaneously pro-Jewish and pro-

Arab seemed likely to be fraught with disaster for all three parties.

By 1931, the Jews still did not form more than 17.7 per cent of the total population of Palestine. But in the early 1930s, Hitler's persecutions began to give rise to a new flood of immigration from Germany, Austria and Poland. In 1939, the Jews numbered 429,605 out of a total population of one and a half million. Meanwhile, tension was rising steadily and by 1936 had reached such a pitch that the growing disorders erupted into actual warfare. The Arab Rebellion had broken out. Armed bands took to the hills, soon to be joined by volunteers from Syria and Iraq. Arrests and internment of the leaders only seemed to intensify the violence; conflicts with the British garrison grew and terrorism was widespread. A general strike began in April 1936 and soon brought about the almost complete stoppage of Arab labour and business activities. For the first time the neighbouring Arab states became active on the Palestine scene. Both the Emir Abdullah of Trans-Jordan and Nuri Said, Foreign Minister of Iraq (whose countries were bound to Britain by treaty and mandatory ties) tried to use their influence to bring about a settlement favourable to the Arabs but which would also be in line with Britain's resolve not to give in to violence. They failed, and finally the British sent an entire division to Palestine and instituted martial law in the little country. Arab intransigence was dampened by the threat of military action and also by the exhaustion of their community's modest resources, owing to the prolonged strike; and when, on 8 October 1936, the Arab Higher Committee, led by Haj Amin el Husseini, Mufti of Jerusalem, received a telegram from King Ibn Saud, asking it in the name of Saudi Arabia, Iraq, Yemen and Trans-Jordan to call off the strike and assuring it of support for the Palestine Arab cause, it was glad of an opportunity to comply. The strike ended on 12 October, and a few days later a Royal Commission, which had been waiting in the wings owing to the disturbed condition of the country, left London for Palestine, under the chairmanship of Lord Peel. Its task was to ascertain the underlying cause of the Arab Revolt and to make recommendations for the removal of 'any legitimate grievances the Arabs or Jews might have'.

When the Royal Commission reported, their proposal was drastic. They found that 'an irrepressible conflict' had broken out between the Arabs and Jews and that their cultural and social life, their ways of thought and conduct were as incompatible as their national aspirations.

The War and its sequel have inspired all Arabs with the hope of reviving in a free and united Arab world the traditions of the Arab golden age. The Jews similarly are inspired by their historic past. They mean to show what the Jewish nation can achieve when restored to the land of its birth. National assimilation between Arabs and Jews is thus ruled out. . . .

The commission went on to conclude that the mandate was unworkable and should be replaced by the division of Palestine into a Jewish and an Arab state (the latter incorporated into Trans-Jordan) and an area under permanent British mandate, to include Jerusalem, Bethlehem, Lydda, Ramleh and a corridor to the sea at Jaffa.

The proposed abrogation of the mandate required a submission to the Council of the League of Nations through its Permanent Mandates Commission. The commission was hurriedly called into special session and heard the Colonial Secretary, William Ormsby-Gore (later Lord Harlech), state that the British government had been driven to the conclusion that the aspirations of the two parties could not be satisfied under the terms of the mandate and that 'a scheme of partition on the general lines recommended by the [Royal] Commission represents the best and most hopeful solution of the deadlock'. The moment of truth had arrived; or, at any rate, so it appeared in 1937.

The Mandates Commission, with its usual expertise and punctiliousness, subjected the Colonial Secretary to a long and gruelling examination, probing into all aspects and repercussions of partition. It was particularly concerned with the probable reaction of the two parties. Mr Ormsby-Gore was rather evasive: the Arabs, he said, feared the future as much as they disliked the present. As for the Jews, it was clear to him that while the Zionist Congress (which was meeting at the time in Zürich) 'wanted this, that and the other and while it complained about the past – as it had done continuously for years – Zionists did not reject a solution on the lines of partition and were thinking constructively about the possibilities of a Jewish state'. The commission in due course informed the League Council that, in its view, the mandate had become 'almost unworkable' and that 'the policy of extreme conciliation pursued hitherto between the two opposing parties has failed of results'. More cautiously, it added that it favoured in principle an examination by the council of the partition solution, but warned against the premature granting of independence to the two states.

The Zionist Congress meanwhile heard Ben Gurion hail the partition proposal as 'One of the greatest acts in history. This is the beginning of redemption for which we have waited 2,000 years.' Weizmann, who understood that the British were no longer willing to enforce the mandate at the expense of constant unrest in Palestine and the growing hostility of the Arab states, also urged the delegates to accept partition, arguing that a small Jewish state would be preferable to minority status within a hostile Arab Palestine; but the congress was deeply divided and eventually adopted a resolution which blew both hot and cold, rejecting the Royal Commission's scheme but authorizing the Zionist Executive to negotiate with the British 'in order to ascertain the precise terms for the proposed establishment of a Jewish state'.

The Arab Higher Committee meanwhile expressed 'its repugnance to the whole of the partition scheme', and even the more moderate faction in Palestine, the National Defence party, stated that partition was incompatible with Arab aspirations and prejudicial to Arab interests.

However, armed with the Mandates Commission's somewhat lukewarm endorsement, Britain on 16 September 1937 asked and received the authorization of the Council of the League to go ahead with a study of the many questions of detail to which partition would give rise. The council did not take any stand on the question of principle. A pan-Arab congress taking place at the same time in Bludan in Syria heard its chairman, a former prime minister of Iraq, describe Zionism as 'a cancer in the body politic' and hint that the Arab states might sever their ties with France and Britain in favour of the other countries.

In the summer of 1938, the skies over Europe were heavy with war clouds. Britain and France were ranged against Germany and Italy over the fate of Czechoslovakia. Once again, the British were to withdraw from a declared position on Palestine. In view of the growing danger of a world war, they had no choice but to seek a settlement in Palestine which would at least not weaken their position in the Arab and Moslem worlds. Apart from all other considerations, they could not afford to alienate the population of a region which contained vital bases, resources and communications. Yet Britain could not abandon the Jews at the very moment when they were threatened by the menace of Hitlerism. The decision was taken to continue a policy of conciliation, but this time one which was heavily weighted against the Jews.

On 18 October 1938 the U.S. Secretary of State, Cordell Hull, issued a statement declaring that the American government and people had watched with the keenest sympathy the development in Palestine of the National Home, but pointing out that the United States was not empowered to prevent any alteration to the mandate. The State Department would, however, 'take all necessary measures for the protection of American rights and interests in Palestine'. President Roosevelt reaffirmed this position a week later. He had, in fact, been receiving a steady barrage of letters, telegrams and visits from influential American Jews urging that rumoured British restrictions on Jewish immigration to Palestine should not take place. Hull duly kept successive American ambassadors in London informed of these pressures, but was careful to instruct the envoys 'to make it entirely clear to the British that we were not in any way questioning Britain's responsibility for Palestine's administration or presuming to interfere in that administration'.

That autumn a British government technical commission (the Woodhead, or Partition, Commission) reported after a visit to Palestine that no plan of partition could be evolved which could offer much hope of successful application. The government was no doubt thankful, in the circumstances, to be able to announce that partition had been found to be unworkable, and that representatives of the Palestine Arabs, the neighbouring Arab states and the Jewish Agency would shortly be invited to London for a conference. If no agreement were reached within a reasonable period, the mandatory power intended to impose a settlement.

The conference met in St James's Palace on 7 February 1939. The Arabs refused to sit with the Jews, and the Mufti's partisans refused to meet the more moderate Palestine Arab representatives. The British delegation had, perforce, to carry on these three simultaneous negotiations. It was obvious from the start that the conference would have no result other than to emphasize, once again, the stubborn opposition between the Arab and Jewish viewpoints.

The British now had to announce their promised plan for a settlement. The White Paper issued on 17 May 1939 by the Secretary of State for the Colonies came as no surprise to the contending parties, for it differed but little from a tentative plan already suggested by the British delegation towards the end of the St James's Palace conference, and promptly rejected by both sides. The White Paper stated that the government would regard it as

> contrary to their obligations to the Arabs under the Mandate, as well as to the assurances which had been given to the Arab people in the past, that the Arab population of Palestine should be made the subjects of a Jewish State against their will.

It proposed that an independent Palestinian state should be established within ten years. Jewish immigration would be limited to 75,000 over a five-year period; by the end of that period, the Jews would constitute one third of the total population and any further immigration would cease unless Arab consent to it could be secured. During the interim period, the sale of land to Jews would be restricted in certain areas and prohibited in others.

Undeterred by the ensuing uproar and by the grudging acceptance of their policy by the House of Commons, where they had only been able to muster 268 votes out of 413, with Winston Churchill and some twenty other government supporters voting against them, the British government once again laid its proposals before the Mandates Commission. For the last time, during eleven arduous meetings, the commission and the Colonial Secretary wrestled with 'the most difficult of all the mandates'. The Jewish National Home, Malcolm MacDonald contended, was already established; the Jews 'had responded magnificently to their opportunity'. But to allow Arab hostility to develop to the point of desperation would be 'to encourage a situation gravely prejudicial to the political and economic security' of the National Home.

The Mandates Commission was not greatly impressed by these arguments. It reported to the League Council that the 1939 White Paper was not in accordance with the interpretation which the commission, the council and the mandatory power itself had hitherto always placed upon the mandate. They suggested that partition still presented the best hope of a settlement and 'should be borne in mind at the appropriate moment.' The commission's views were only advisory and the British prepared to lay their case before the council in early September. But by that time the Second World War had broken out and the League of Nations would soon vanish as a political force. The legal status of the White Paper was never to be clarified. But, from then on, the British governed Palestine in accordance with its terms and without the consent of either section of the population.

2. THE ZIONISTS FIGHT BACK

Balfour's 'adventure' had seemingly come to a tragic end. At the very moment when the Nazi persecution of the European Jews began, the doors of Palestine were closed in their faces and the Jews already there found themselves, in Winston Churchill's words, trapped in 'one more precarious Oriental ghetto'. For the Zionists and the entire Jewish world, the 'Palestine Munich', as its critics in the British Labour party called the 1939 White Paper, was a betrayal, an exercise in appeasement, a sacrifice of the weak by the strong. For them, and for many of its non-Jewish opponents, it recalled the fate of Abyssinia, the capitulation of the British and French to the Axis Powers at Munich and the fall of Czechoslovakia. The Twenty-first Zionist Congress declared in August 1939 that 'The Jewish people will not acquiesce in the reduction of its status in Palestine to that of a minority, nor in the subjection of a Jewish National Home to Arab rule.' In America, Justice Brandeis issued a statement declaring that a legal obligation assumed by Great Britain was the basis for 'Jewish construction enterprise in Palestine. That legal right, sustained by humanitarian needs, cannot be obliterated for private advantage.'

Though some Arab leaders recognized that an important advance had been made towards recognizing their basic claims, and the Chief Minister of Trans-Jordan, Tawfiq Abu-al-Huda, stated publicly that 'a new era of co-operation between the British and the Arabs of Palestine' might now be in sight, the Arab Higher Committee promptly repudiated the White Paper altogether.

In deciding the fate of a living nation [the Committee stated], 'the last word does not rest with White or Black Papers; it is the will of the nation itself that decides its future. The Arab people will reach the desired goal: Palestine shall be independent within an Arab Federation and shall remain forever Arab.'

Predictably a flood of American Zionist protests poured into the Department of State and prompted a majority of the House Foreign Affairs Committee, together with twenty-eight Senators, publicly to protest against the British clamp-down on immigration; to describe the defence of Jewish interests in Palestine as a moral obligation of the United States; and to claim that the 1939 White Paper violated the 1924 Anglo-American Convention. An analysis of the White Paper had been prepared for President Roosevelt by his Secretary of State, Cordell Hull, and the President commented:

I have read with interest and a good deal of dismay the decisions of the British government regarding its Palestine policy. Frankly, I do not believe that the British are wholly correct in saying that the framers of the Palestine mandate 'could not have intended that Palestine should be converted into a Jewish state against the will of the Arab population of the country'. My recollection is that this way of putting it is deceptive for the reason that while the Palestine mandate undoubtedly did not intend to take away the right of citizenship and of taking part in the government on the part of the Arab population, it nevertheless did intend to convert

24

Palestine into a Jewish home which might very possibly become preponderantly Jewish within a comparatively short time. . . . My offhand thought is that while there are some good ideas in regard to actual administration of government in this new White Paper, it is something that we cannot give approval to by the United States.

Roosevelt's own contribution to ideas for a settlement was that at the end of five years the whole problem should be re-examined and, at that time, either permanently settled or else that arrangements should be made for the existing régime to continue for a further five years. A year or two later he was inclined to favour an international trusteeship, turning Palestine into a real Holy Land for Judaism, Islam and Christianity.*

The President did not wish his views on the White Paper to be communicated to the British, and the State Department merely cabled the ambassador in London, Joseph Kennedy, instructing him to mention, informally and orally, the widespread disappointment in America, especially in Zionist circles, over certain of the White Paper's provisions.

Despite the shock of the 1939 White Paper, the Jewish Agency at the outbreak of the Second World War immediately issued a declaration of loyal support for Britain. Jewish terrorism, which had been growing in Palestine since the publication of the White Paper, stopped completely and an illegal radio station closed down. But, only a few weeks later, Ben Gurion defined the paramount goals of Zionism as 'the continuation and increase of Jewish immigration' and 'the extension of our land possessions'; while in New York Weizmann assured a Zionist meeting that he was convinced the White Paper was not the last word of British statesman-

* The State Department studied this idea, but came to the conclusion that in the absence of a friendly background against which the parties could meet, it would be inopportune to 'stir the sands of Palestine' at that juncture.

ship. They should be on guard to take advantage of any circumstance that might lead London to repudiate it.

Ever since the Royal Commission had made its partition proposals in 1937, based to a large extent on the density of Jewish settlement in certain areas of Palestine, the Jewish National Fund had been laying more stress than formerly on political and strategic considerations in their land purchase programme. The President of the Fund in the United States told a conference in Washington early in 1940 that the policy of the fund had been to forestall as far as possible the geographical basis for possible partition or cantonization by purchasing areas on the frontiers; and Dr Bernard Joseph, the legal adviser to the Jewish Agency, later announced to a Canadian Zionist Convention that 'eight new settlements were set up in the first year of the war . . . in the places that are on the outskirts, in order to secure, when the day comes, that the whole of Palestine will be Jewish and not only part of it'.

Although the great majority of Zionists had always tacitly aimed at a Jewish state, most of their leaders had found it expedient, so long as Britain was allowing the National Home to be built up gradually, to soft-pedal their real objective; but the White Paper was a watershed. From then on, the emphasis shifted openly to their true political goal. Among the resolutions adopted by a conference organized in January 1941 in Washington by the United Palestine Appeal, and attended by over 2,000 American Zionists, was one calling for the establishment of Palestine as a Jewish Commonwealth; and in September of that year the Zionist Organization of America demanded the reconstruction of Palestine 'within its historic boundaries as a Jewish Commonwealth'. Two months later, Dr Nahum Goldmann, then chief of the administrative committee of the World Jewish Congress, defined the extent of that commonwealth as the whole of Palestine, and added that the Zionists must demand the extension of their activities to Trans-Jordan, even if the status of that country should be different from that of Palestine.

In all this, Zionist thinking did not entirely neglect the

Arabs. 'We should say to the Arab peoples,' declared the labour leader Berl Katznelson, 'we are ready to aid your efforts towards unity and independence if you will cease to trouble us and if you will recognize Palestine as a Jewish state. On such a basis it is possible to achieve mutual understanding and co-operation.' A typically Zionist conception of mutual aid and understanding, as Professor G. E. Kirk has pointed out in his book on *The Middle East in the War*, and one which was to be echoed later by Ben Gurion when he addressed the United Nations Special Committee on Palestine.

For his part, Ben Gurion clearly foresaw that at the end of the war European Judaism would be shattered and the supporters of Zionism greatly weakened. A new and powerful ally had to be won for the Zionist cause – the Government of the United States – and this could not be achieved without enrolling American Jewry in a wholehearted and dynamic campaign. The greatest concern of Palestine Jewish leaders was, he wrote,

> the fate of Palestine after the war. I was convinced of the necessity to establish a Jewish state. It already appeared evident that the British would not keep their mandate. While there was every reason that Hitler would be defeated, it seemed equally obvious that Britain, even though victorious, would be considerably weakened by the war. However willing, she would not be strong enough to exercise a new mandate, or carry out the project of partition in the face of all the Arab countries. For my part, I had no doubt that the centre of gravity of our political efforts had shifted from Great Britain to America, who was making sure of being the world's leading power and where the greatest number of Jews – as well as the most influential – were to be found.

Ben Gurion saw that this could only be achieved by 'thinking big', by presenting Americans with a simple and dramatic programme. This reasoning lay at the back of what came to be known as the Biltmore Programme. There had to be a break – and a decisive one – with gradualism, the reliance on the

British, on slow and delicate negotiations – in short, with the moderate view personified by Weizmann. Hitherto Ben Gurion and Weizmann had agreed on goals and had disagreed solely on tactics. Now the break was complete.

At the beginning of 1942, Ben Gurion, then in the United States, drew up a memorandum which virtually stated the case for a Jewish state. Both history and international law, he wrote, had designated Palestine as a National Home for the Jewish people. Under the mandatory régime, indifferent if not hostile to Zionist goals, the Jews in their enthusiasm and pioneering spirit had been able to expand the capacity of the country so that it could absorb large numbers of immigrants; therefore after the war, if a régime were in power dedicated to welcoming and settling the immigrants, Palestine could absorb as many Jews as could come. Such a régime could only be a Jewish government. 'To secure a homeland for homeless Jews, the Jews themselves must be entrusted with its reconstruction.'

Some American Zionist leaders found the memorandum premature, but Justice Felix Frankfurter supported it and undertook to get it to President Roosevelt. After the document had gone to the White House, Ben Gurion circulated copies to all the leaders of the Zionist movement in the United States and it formed the basis of the Biltmore Programme.

In May 1942, at a highly dangerous period for the Allies on the Far Eastern, the Middle Eastern and the Russian Fronts, 600 American Zionists and sixty-seven Zionists from other countries met in conference in the Biltmore Hotel in New York. Almost every shade of Zionist opinion was represented, and some non-Zionists were also present. The meeting was organized by the American Committee for Zionist Affairs, but Ben Gurion was its moving spirit. The three-day conference took place at a bitter moment in Jewish history. The participants were deeply moved by the plight of Europe's Jews and indignant at what they naturally saw as the cold and cruel British refusal to allow unlimited Jewish immigration to Palestine; they were still suffering under the shock of the recent *Struma* disaster, when 768 refugees from Europe bound for Palestine had been drowned,* and they fiercely resented the continuing British refusal to comply with the Zionist demand for a Jewish fighting force under its own flag.

Ben Gurion made an inspiring speech.

> Our past works and achievements in Palestine [he declared] have a double contribution to make to the reshaping of human society and the remaking of Jewish history. They will serve as the pedestal on which to build the Jewish Commonwealth. ... To build it will need maximal effort by the entire Jewish people, in the Diaspora and in Palestine. As part of the great human cause, America, England, Russia and other nations that champion humanity may be expected to help us. But we must do the job ourselves. Palestine will be as Jewish as the Jews will make it.

Though he maintained a dignified silence, Weizmann bitterly resented the fact that Ben Gurion, in his campaign to get his programme adopted, did not hesitate to make use of an article on 'Palestine's Role in the Solution of the Jewish Problem' which Weizmann himself had published in the January 1942 issue of *Foreign Affairs*. 'The Arabs must be clearly told,' Weizmann had written, 'that the Jews will be encouraged to settle in Palestine and will control their own immigration; that here Jews who so desire will be able to achieve their freedom and self-government by establishing a state of their own.' Weizmann had intended his article as a statement of long-term aims, and he was indignant that Ben Gurion had, for his own purposes, drafted a resolution which did not depart from Weizmann's meaning but which gave it a more pressing and extremist ring, thereby endangering and perhaps ruining Weizmann's pending negotiations with the British for a Jewish armed force.

* In late 1941, the s.s. *Struma*, a cattle-ship, sailed from a port in the Balkans, overloaded with illegal immigrants for Palestine and thoroughly unseaworthy. Her engines broke down off the Turkish coast and she was held up. During negotiations between the British and the Turks for the landing of the children on board, the Turkish government ordered the ship to return to the port whence she had sailed. She sank in a heavy storm on 23 February 1942. Only one passenger survived.

Under Ben Gurion's leadership, the conference adopted eight resolutions, the last three of which came to be known as the Biltmore Programme, the first official declaration of Jewish statehood as World Zionism's post-war aim.

... 6. The Conference calls for the fulfilment of the original purpose of the Balfour Declaration and the Mandate which *recognizing the historical connection of the Jewish people with Palestine* was to afford them the opportunity, as stated by President Wilson, to found there a Jewish Commonwealth.

The Conference affirms its unalterable rejection of the White Paper of May 1939 and denies its moral or legal validity. The White Paper seeks to limit, and in fact to nullify Jewish rights to immigration and settlement in Palestine and, as stated by Mr Winston Churchill in the House of Commons in May 1939, 'constitutes a breach and repudiation of the Balfour Declaration'. The policy of the White Paper is cruel and indefensible in its denial of sanctuary to Jews fleeing from Nazi persecution; and at a time when Palestine has become a focal point in the war front of the United Nations, and Palestine Jewry must provide all available manpower for farm and factory and camp, it is in direct conflict with the interests of the allied war effort.

7. In the struggle against the forces of aggression and tyranny, of which Jews were the earliest victims, and which now menace the Jewish National Home, recognition must be given to the right of the Jews of Palestine to play their full part in the war effort and in the defence of their country, through a Jewish military force fighting under its own flag and under the high command of the United Nations.

8. The Conference declares that the new world order that will follow victory cannot be established on foundations of peace, justice and equality, unless the problem of Jewish homelessness is finally solved.

The Conference urges that the gates of Palestine be

opened; that the Jewish Agency be vested with control of immigration into Palestine and with the necessary authority for upbuilding the country, including the development of its unoccupied and uncultivated lands; and that Palestine be established as a Jewish Commonwealth integrated in the structure of the new democratic world.

Then and only then will the age-old wrong to the Jewish people be righted.

The mandatory power's wartime censorship system saw to it that not one word of these inflammable sentiments reached Palestine through the press or radio.

The Biltmore resolutions were adopted without a dissenting vote, but they did not represent an outright victory because the American Jewish Committee, a body believed to have much political influence, had not taken part in the conference, and one faction of Ben Gurion's own political party, the Mapai, opposed the Biltmore Programme on the grounds that it would only lead to partition. But the resolutions were technically unopposed, and in November 1942 the Action Committee of the Zionist General Council – the most authoritative Zionist body at the time, since neither the Zionist Congress nor its General Council could meet because of the war – adopted the Biltmore Programme in Jerusalem by twenty-one votes to four.

American Zionists had received the guiding principles they needed for a new and vigorous action campaign; but they realized that an essential first step was to secure the backing of the American Jewish community as a whole. It would be fatal if the general public in America felt that the Jews themselves were divided on fundamental issues. The task was not easy, and it was not until August 1943 that the American Jewish Conference was convened. The conference was broadly based but Zionist-dominated – of the 300 elected delegates, 240 were formal members of the Zionist Organization of America and its affiliates.

Judge Joseph M. Proskauer, President of the American Jewish Committee and a justice of the New York State Supreme Court, called for continued immigration into Palestine; but Dr Abba Hillel Silver urged that American Jewish unity be built on the stronger plank of Jewish statehood. In vain Proskauer warned that all those hostile to Jewry 'are just waiting for the urging of these maximum demands in order to cement the opposition to the legitimate building up of Palestine itself'. It would be a tragedy to put forth these demands, he contended. But, at Silver's insistence, the conference enthusiastically adopted the Biltmore Programme, by a vote of 478 to four, with nineteen abstentions. The Zionist objective of organizing American Jewry behind its programme – or rather, the great majority of organized Jewish groups, representing, according to Zionist claims, 90 per cent of the whole community – had been attained. The next step, as the President of the Zionist Organization of America, Rabbi Israel Goldstein, declared, was to 'win the wholehearted approval of the American Government and people for the Zionist program with respect to Palestine, which has now become the program of the whole of American Jewry through the democratically elected American Jewish Conference'.

All this was happening against a background of supreme tragedy. On 24 November 1942 Rabbi Stephen Wise, President of the American Jewish Congress, announced that the State Department had substantiated information, received from American Jewish organizations, that Hitler had ordered the extermination of all Jews in occupied territories before the end of the year and that some two million had already perished or had been deported. A day of mourning was observed by Jews throughout the world on 2 December. Then came the sombre announcement issued by all the Allied governments on 17 December 1942:

From all the occupied countries Jews are being transported in conditions of appalling horror and brutality, to Eastern Europe. . . . None of those taken away are ever heard of again. The able-bodied are slowly worked to death in labour camps. The infirm are left to die of exposure and starvation or are deliberately massacred in mass executions.

The number of victims of these bloody cruelties is reckoned in many hundreds of thousands of entirely innocent men, women and children.

The campaign for a Jewish state in Palestine which the Zionist leadership in America now launched was one of the most brilliant and successful of such efforts ever to have taken place, even if account is taken of the entire absence of a comparable counter-campaign by the Arabs and of the ignorance of nearly all American public figures and ordinary citizens that the state they were being asked to endorse was to be established in a country belonging to another people – the Palestine Arabs. Large-scale Jewish immigration from Europe to Palestine was now tragically irrelevant – Nahum Goldmann was to tell the Twenty-second World Zionist Congress in 1946 that the Biltmore Programme had been drawn up on the assumption that millions of Jews would be transferred to Palestine immediately after the war – and the emphasis was on the need to save the remnant of Jewry and on the fact that a Jewish state was a world need and a just compensation for innumerable oppressions and massacres suffered in the past.

The campaign soon became effective. The American press was supplied with a flow of press releases, and by 1945, 25 per cent of them were appearing in national newspapers. Brilliant use was also made of the Zionists' close personal relations with the press and radio worlds. The Public Relations Department of the Zionist Organization kept closely in touch with the leading Washington correspondents of the national press. Zionist press conferences in Washington and New York were imposing affairs, attended by correspondents representing all the major press associations and radio networks.

In 1943–4 alone, over a million leaflets and pamphlets were distributed to public libraries, community centres, clergymen, teachers and writers. Among the books by non-Jewish authors subsidized by the Zionists and promoted by them, jointly with professional publishers, were the Rev. Norman MacLean's *His Terrible Swift Sword*, Professor Carl J. Friedrich's *American Policy towards Palestine*, Frank Gervasi's

To Whom Palestine, and Dr Walter Clay Lowdermilk's *Palestine, Land of Promise*, a book that reached the best-seller lists.

Astute use was made of the practice of associating important public figures with the Zionist cause, and a special effort was directed to winning the support of organized Christianity. An American Palestine Committee was formed, with the Senator for New York, Robert F. Wagner, as its chairman, Monsignor John F. Ryan as its vice-chairman, and a board which included many celebrated figures, among them Senators Taft and Vandenbergh, William Green, President of the American Federation of Labor, and Harold Ickes, Secretary of the Interior. The committee's first public action was to sponsor a declaration backing 'the restoration of Jews in Palestine' and emphasizing 'the tragic plight of refugees fleeing from persecution and finding no home'. The Zionists realized that, while many Americans could not be roused to enthusiasm for a Jewish state, it was easy to exploit American generosity and humanitarianism for Zionist ends by stressing the despair of the refugees.

Considerable use was made of huge mass meetings and protest rallies, notably after Dr Silver became co-chairman, with Dr Stephen Wise, of the American Zionist Emergency Council, into which the American Emergency Council for Zionist Affairs had been transformed. Though the techniques and atmosphere of these meetings sometimes had a disturbing similarity to similar demonstrations in Nazi Germany, Silver favoured them because he held that, in a democracy, public opinion determines government action in the final analysis and large meetings were a dramatic way of involving the general public and highlighting public enthusiasm for a cause. 'Talk to the whole of America,' he adjured his fellow-Zionists, 'make friends everywhere; carry on an active educational propaganda in your circle, within the sphere of your influence, among your own friends. That will sustain them when they come to make important decisions which may involve America's participation in the ultimate solution of the Palestine problem.'

The first major project was a massive campaign against the 1939 White Paper. Local committees were directed to establish contacts with their congressmen and community and state government representatives, in order to familiarize them with details of Palestine, as seen from the Zionist standpoint; and, at appropriate moments, to deluge congressmen, senators and public officials with letters and telegrams. Hundreds of thousands of individual letters, postcards and cabled petitions in fact reached Washington during the campaign. Radio time was purchased on 182 American and fifty Canadian stations, and famous screen stars appeared in dramatizations on the theme 'Palestine speaks'. As a result of the anti-White Paper campaign, the governors of forty states sent an eloquent petition to the President urging the establishment of a Jewish state; and trade unions, church groups and such important associations as Rotary, Lions and Elks went on record as wholeheartedly opposing the White Paper.

Zionist efforts now turned towards Washington and the task of securing the introduction of Palestine resolutions into both houses of Congress.

3. GROWING
INVOLVEMENT

Already by late 1942, Zionist agitation centring on the Biltmore Declaration had begun to cause grave anxiety in Arab capitals. Nuri Said, the Prime Minister of Iraq, and Mohamad Ali, the heir to the throne of Egypt, protested to the American Ambassadors in Baghdad and Cairo about pro-Zionist statements emanating from the United States. The Egyptian minister in Washington handed the Secretary of State an *aide-mémoire* calling attention to 'the deplorable effect on the Arab and Moslem world of Zionist activities and their possible repercussions on the Allied war effort'. In a message to President Roosevelt, sent in April 1943, followed by a letter dispatched in May, King Ibn Saud of Saudi Arabia explained that, although pressed to make representations to the President, he had refrained from such action because he did not wish to embarrass the United States in a period of war crisis or to prejudice the Allied cause by doing anything to increase Arab-Jewish antagonism. He asked Roosevelt to give him advance information of any steps of an affirmative character contemplated by the American government with respect to Palestine. Not only in Zionist minds, but in wider circles, it had begun to be taken for granted that the United States would, henceforth, play a preponderant role in Middle Eastern problems.

In a reply dated 26 May 1943, the President voiced his appreciation of the King's sympathetic understanding. He added that, if a friendly understanding on Palestine should be reached by the Arabs and Jews through their own efforts during the war, such a development would be considered highly desirable by the United States; in any event, it was the view of the American government that 'no decision altering the basic situation of Palestine should be reached without fully consulting with both Jews and Arabs'. Roosevelt's response to Ibn Saud was the first occasion on which the United States assumed active responsibility in the Palestine problem.

In June 1943 Colonel Harold B. Hoskins was sent to Saudi Arabia at the President's direction to ask the King whether he would enter into discussions on the future of Palestine with Dr Weizmann or some representative selected by the Jewish Agency. Colonel Hoskins, a Middle East expert who had, the year before, visited the region on a mission for the Joint Chiefs of Staff and who had since made clear his view that an Arab-Jewish armed conflict might break out unless something were rapidly done to ease tensions, cannot have been surprised at Ibn Saud's response. The King turned the suggestion down, pointing out that he could not speak for Palestine, much less 'deliver it to the Jews', even if he were for an instant willing to consider such a proposal.

Meanwhile a gigantic refugee problem had been building up in Europe, where the refugees from Germany and Nazi-occupied countries numbered several millions, including thousands of Jews. One of Roosevelt's great hopes was that immigration barriers against the Jews might be lifted by all countries, including the United States. In April 1943, America and Britain jointly sponsored the Bermuda Refugee Conference, which revived the Inter-governmental Committee on Refugees, with the aim of finding countries of refuge for all categories of displaced persons who could not be repatriated.

To avoid involvement in political controversy, Palestine was expressly excluded from the committee's activities. This was enough to prompt the Zionists to boycott and attack the committee and even Roosevelt's personal initiatives to further its aims. There was not only the fund-raising factor, which Roosevelt recognized and understood: if Palestine was not, in fact, the only solution to the Jewish problem, as the Zionists insisted, the whole basis of their programme would be jeopardized. Above all, the more extreme American Zionist leaders looked on Jewish refugees, no matter how tragic their plight as individuals, only as potential citizens of a Jewish state. Dr Silver was, in fact, to tell the Twenty-second World Zionist Congress in December 1946 – the first to meet after the war – that

> Zionism is not an immigration or a refugee movement, but a movement to re-establish the Jewish State for a Jewish nation in the land of Israel. The classic textbook of Zionism is not how to find a home for refugees. The classic textbook of our movement is *The Jewish State*.

Early in 1944, the State Department learned to its dismay that, at the instigation of the Zionists, resolutions based on the Biltmore Programme were being introduced into both Houses of Congress. They stated that,

> The United States shall use its good offices and take appropriate measures to the end that the doors of Palestine shall be opened for free entry of Jews into that country and that there shall be full opportunity for colonization so that the Jewish people may ultimately reconstitute Palestine as a free and democratic Jewish commonwealth.

Public hearings were held early in February by the House Committee on Foreign Relations, under the chairmanship of Sol Bloom, a recognized Zionist spokesman in the House of Representatives. The American Zionist Emergency Committee saw to it that the congressmen were deluged with a flood of letters and telegrams from members of the public. Opinion in both Houses was reportedly unanimous that seldom had such an 'amazing public interest' been taken in a piece of legislation. Bloom had himself assembled a book of documents to 'guide' the members of his committee. It included certain key documents, but was largely made up of anti-White Paper statements made by British statesmen in 1939.

Apart from all other considerations, the State Department feared that the resolutions might ruin pending negotiations with Ibn Saud for the construction of an oil pipeline across Saudi Arabia, which the American military leaders believed to be vital for the security of the United States. As the department foresaw, immediate protests poured in from the governments of Egypt, Iraq and Lebanon as well as from King Ibn Saud and the Imam Yahya of Yemen. Washington countered as best it could with explanations that the resolutions, even if passed, were not binding on the executive, and Roosevelt hastened to renew his assurances to Ibn Saud that the American government's view remained that no decision should be taken changing Palestine's status without full prior consultation with both Arabs and Jews. Similar statements were addressed to the Imam and to the Egyptian government.

While the State Department was wondering how to persuade both Houses of Congress to refrain from taking action on the resolutions, Stimson, the Secretary of War, informed Senator Connally, Chairman of the Senate Committee on Foreign Relations, that the resolution before the Senate was a matter of deep concern to his department, since its passage, or even public hearings on it, might have dangerous repercussions in the Middle East, an area of vital military interest to the United States. General Marshall, who had sounded out the opinions of American military attachés in the Middle East, testified to the committee in this sense in secret session. The State Department's view that the resolutions were inopportune was also explained to Connally. So the resolutions were shelved, to the great relief of the responsible officials concerned. Had they been passed, they might for the first time have involved the United States in active support for Zionism.

However, it seemed that any involvement, however remote,

in the Palestine issue on the part of an American president inevitably led to conflicting expressions of policy. Just as Woodrow Wilson had with one hand approved the Balfour Declaration and with the other dispatched the King–Crane Commission to report on the views on the future of Palestine – well known to be anti-Zionist – of the people of the country, so Roosevelt gave an interview on 9 March 1944 to Dr Wise and Dr Silver, authorizing them (according to press reports) to announce that 'when future decisions are reached, full justice will be done to those who seek a Jewish National Home'; that the United States had never given its approval to the White Paper of 1939; and that the President was 'happy that the doors of Palestine are today open to Jewish refugees'. (In Cordell Hull's view, it was owing to United States concern that the British had decided not to terminate Jewish immigration into Palestine after 31 March 1944, as laid down in the White Paper, arguing that because of war conditions the quota for the preceding five years had not been filled by about 30,000 permits.)

Once again the State Department had the awkward task of explaining away reported statements. Nahas Pasha, the Prime Minister of Egypt, had to be told that the press reports of the President's statements were substantially accurate. The United States missions in Cairo and Baghdad were instructed to point out, however, that the President had referred to a National Home rather than to the Commonwealth invoked in the Congressional resolutions; that the American government had never taken a position on the White Paper; and that the assurances regarding consultations of Arabs and Jews were still valid.

Cordell Hull later wrote that Rabbis Wise and Silver believed that the President had made pledges to them. He added drily 'the State Department made no pledges'. In any event, the President's statement to the two Zionist leaders marked the beginning of a new situation; henceforth, American policy on Palestine tended to be fashioned in the White House, sometimes without the advice of the War, Navy and State Departments and more frequently against that advice; for the opposition of these departments to United States support for Zionism was to continue and, if anything, become stronger. It became clear to them that the fulfilment of Zionist goals would jeopardize America's position in the post-war Middle East, for it would disrupt the Arab world and pave the way for infiltration by Soviet Russia.

As a result of assiduous Zionist efforts, both the Democratic and the Republican platforms in the 1944 election contained planks calling for unrestricted Jewish immigration into Palestine and the constitution of the country as a Jewish Commonwealth; and, during a convention of the Zionist Organization of America in October, a letter from President Roosevelt was read out in which he quoted the Democratic plank and added:

Efforts will be made to find effective ways and means of effectuating this policy as soon as practicable. I know how long and ardently the Jewish people have worked and prayed for the establishment of Palestine as a free and democratic Jewish Commonwealth. I am convinced that the American people give their support to this aim and if re-elected I shall help to bring about its realization.

Just about this time a very different note was being struck by the British in Palestine. On 10 October 1944 the High Commissioner and the Commander in Chief, Middle East Forces, jointly issued an official announcement castigating the outrages and crimes of violence which had, since early 1944, been carried out by 'Jewish terrorists acting with the deliberate intention of bringing about by force developments favourable to the realization of their political aims'. These events, the communiqué continued, were proceeding side by side with

the bitterest phase of the critical fight between the United Nations and Nazi Germany – the cruellest, most implacable and most ruthless persecution that the long history of Jewry has ever known. Criminals in Palestine, with their active and passive sympathizers, are directly impeding the war effort.

41

A few months later, with the election safely over, President Roosevelt, on his way to the Yalta Conference, confided to Winston Churchill over luncheon his intention of visiting King Ibn Saud on his way home in order to discuss the Palestine question with him. Byrnes, as Secretary of State, was also present at the luncheon, and later commented that the President 'wanted to bring about peace between the Arabs and Jews. Churchill wished him good luck but didn't seem very hopeful that the President would meet with success. He didn't.'

On his return from his meeting with Ibn Saud, Roosevelt told Congress that he had learned more about the whole problem by talking with Ibn Saud for five minutes than he could have learned in an exchange of two or three dozen letters. To Edward R. Stettinius he said that he felt

> he must have a conference with Congressional leaders and re-examine our entire policy on Palestine. He was now convinced, he added, that if nature took its course there would be bloodshed between Arabs and Jews. Some formula not yet discovered would have to be evolved to prevent this warfare.

One of Roosevelt's last acts of statehood was to renew, only a week before his death, his assurance to Ibn Saud that the United States wished no decision on the basic situation in Palestine to be taken without full consultation of both Arabs and Jews. The King would doubtless recall, the President added, that 'During our recent conversation I assured you that I would take no action, in my capacity as Chief of the Executive Branch of this Government, which might prove hostile to the Arab people.'

With the death of Roosevelt, followed a few months later by the electoral victory of the Labour party in Britain, two figures whom the wartime world had ranked among the greatest leaders were replaced by men of a very different stamp. And with the end of the war in Europe, Britain, as the Power still in control in Palestine, and the United States, as the recognized leader of the Western world, could no longer put off an attempt to come to grips with the stubborn and tragic Palestine problem.

Harry S. Truman took over from his predecessor a seemingly inextricable maze of conflicting sympathies and contradictory pledges; while Clement Attlee replaced in Churchill a man who, for long a self-styled Zionist (though a highly unusual and unorthodox one), had declared to the House of Commons in November 1944:

> If our dreams for Zionism are to end in the smoke of assassins' pistols and our labours for its future to produce only a new set of gangsters worthy of Nazi Germany, many like myself will have to reconsider the position we have maintained so consistently and so long in the past.

Among the first papers that the new American president found on his desk was a brief prepared by the Department of State warning him that efforts would probably soon be made by Zionist leaders to obtain from him a commitment in favour of their programme for a Jewish state, and urging him to recognize that the whole subject of Palestine was 'one that should be handled with the greatest care and with a view to the long-range interests' of the United States. In the event, President Truman's first week in office was barely over when he received a visit from Dr Stephen Wise, to whom he readily gave assurances that he would do everything he could to carry out President Roosevelt's commitments regarding a Jewish commonwealth.

Attlee, together with his Foreign Secretary, Ernest Bevin, and many others in London, saw with annoyance in the President's pro-Zionist attitude merely the tactics made necessary by the exigencies of American domestic politics. In fact, it represented a sincere conviction, arising largely from his close association with his 'wartime buddy' and later business partner, Eddie Jacobson. The fate of the Jewish displaced persons in Europe and of those Jews already in Palestine was a matter of 'deep personal concern' to Mr Truman. The Balfour Declaration, as he saw it, was a promise which should be kept, 'just as all promises made by responsible, civilized governments should be kept'. The Declaration had always seemed to him 'to go hand in hand with the noble policies of Woodrow Wilson, especially the principle of self-determination'. Despite the preoccupations of the 'striped-pant boys' in the State Department, the President genuinely believed that world peace would best be served in the long run by a solution that would accord justice to the needs and wants of the Jewish people.

That the Balfour Declaration made promises to the Arabs as well as the Jews had doubtless never occurred to him, or, for that matter, to the vast majority of Americans; but he had been briefed on his predecessor's assurances to the Arab leaders concerning consultations, and when the then Egyptian Prime Minister, Nokrashy Pasha, explained to him that the Arabs felt that 'guests at their table were now announcing that they were going to bring in large numbers of their kinsmen, take over Arab lands, and rule to suit themselves', he merely renewed the promise of prior consultations. In his opinion, apparently, the 'noble principle' of self-determination should also apply to the Arabs, but would adequately be carried out if Arabs, as well as Jews, were consulted about a pledge to deprive them, on behalf of the Zionists, of their country and their nationhood.

The President brushed aside with equal aplomb the views of his own experts – a fact which caused considerable annoyance in London, where much comfort had been derived from the knowledge that the State Department thought internationally and that its attitude on Palestine largely coincided with that of the Foreign Office.

Dean Acheson, then Under-Secretary of State, observed that at that time the President's views centred exclusively upon two points: first, immediate immigration into Palestine of 100,000 displaced Jews from Eastern Europe; secondly, the determination to assume no political or military responsibility for this decision. It was the latter point that particularly infuriated Attlee and Bevin and, indeed, most British people with any knowledge of the Middle East. Their sense of frustration was later summed up by Churchill when he declared in the House of Commons that

> an unfair burden was being thrown upon Great Britain by our having to bear the whole weight of the Zionist policy while Arabs and Moslems ... then so important to our Empire, were alarmed and estranged and while the United States and other countries sat on the sidelines and criticized our shortcomings with all the freedom of perfect detachment and irresponsibility.

Attlee, whose view of the National Home, to say nothing of a Jewish state, was that it had been 'a wild experiment that was bound to cause trouble', found a memorandum from Truman on his desk the very day he became prime minister in July 1945. The President hoped that the British might find it possible to lift the White Paper restrictions on Jewish immigration and asked Attlee's views on a settlement of the Palestine problem. Truman added that he looked forward to discussing the problem in concrete terms in the near future.

The figure of 100,000 immigrants was first proposed in a petition from the Jewish Agency to the mandatory power and had been taken up by Mr Earl G. Harrison, Dean of the University of Pennsylvania Law School, who in June 1945 had at the President's request undertaken an investigation of 'non-repatriable' displaced persons in Europe. Harrison's report was submitted in late August, and a few days later the President wrote at length to Attlee, enclosing a copy of the report and urging that the main solution of the problem of the displaced persons in Europe lay in the quick evacuation of as many Jews as possible to Palestine. In his cabled reply, Attlee tried to put the problem in its world setting. The camps contained people from almost every race in Europe and the Allied Control Commission in Germany, he said, was trying to avoid treating concentration camp victims on a racial basis; if the Jews, who were not living in worse conditions than other victims of Nazi persecution, were to be given preference, there would be violent reactions from other groups. Regarding immediate relief measures, two camps in North Africa could take 35,000 Jews. As regards Palestine, it would be very unwise to disregard undertakings by Churchill, Roosevelt and Truman himself that Arabs would be consulted before a final decision was taken on its fate. The Jews had not taken up the available immigration certificates, preferring a solution *à l'outrance* and the complete repudiation of the White Paper, regardless of the effect on the Middle East as a whole. Finally, Britain was at that moment undertaking delicate negotiations concerning her withdrawal from India and had to take into consideration the views and emotions of that country's huge Moslem population. Meanwhile, Attlee concluded, the British were considering a long-term policy which they proposed to refer to the United Nations as soon as practicable and he hoped to inform Truman shortly of British intentions regarding the immigration problem.

The next move was a formal British proposal that an Anglo-American Committee of Inquiry be set up to examine the possibility of immigration of Jews to countries outside Europe, Palestine being considered as only one of the 'countries of disposal'. As soon as the idea of the inquiry became known, the President received a telegram from the American Zionist leadership urging that he should reject the idea of yet another commission 'at a continued cost in human life and human misery' and insist on the immediate admission to Palestine of 100,000 Jews. After talks in Washington in November 1945, Attlee reluctantly fell in with Truman's condition that the United States would only take part in the inquiry if Palestine were considered as its focus. The President announced the formation of the committee on 13 November and on the same day released the text of his letter of 31 August calling for the admission of 100,000 Jews.

In mid-December, both Houses of Congress finally passed the Zionist-sponsored resolution, which had been twice postponed through administration pressure.* This time the Con-

* The second occasion had been in the autumn of 1944, just after the presidential election; the State Department had said that the passage of the resolution would be 'unwise from the standpoint of the general international situation'.

gress overrode objections from both Byrnes and the President himself, each of whom urged that no action be taken until the committee had submitted its recommendations. The resolution read:

> *Resolved by the Senate (the House of Representatives concurring),* that the interest shown by the President in the solution of this problem is hereby commended and that the United States shall use its good offices with the mandatory power to the end that Palestine shall be opened for the free entry of Jews into that country to the maximum of its agricultural and economic potentialities, and that there shall be full opportunity for colonization and development, so that they may freely proceed with the upbuilding of Palestine as the Jewish National Home and, in association with all elements of the population, establish Palestine as a democratic commonwealth in which all men, regardless of race or creed, shall have equal rights.

When it reported in April 1946, the committee rejected the exclusive claims of both Jews and Arabs to Palestine, which should be neither a Jewish nor an Arab State, but one which guarded the rights and interests of Moslems, Jews and Christians alike; and recommended that the form of government to be established should fully protect and preserve the interests in the Holy Land of the three great religions. Specifically the commissioners suggested the continuation of the mandate and the ultimate placing of the country under United Nations trusteeship, and steps to bridge the gap between standards of living and education of the two communities. They expressed the view that the Jewish Agency should co-operate with the mandatory power in suppressing terrorism and illegal immigration, but recommended the cancellation of the White Paper's land transfer regulations and the immediate authorization of 100,000 certificates to Jews and their award as far as possible in 1946. The report contained no word of how these objectives were to be attained.

The Anglo-American Committee's report was made public simultaneously in Washington and London on 1 May 1946.

On that day President Truman – without prior notice to the British, and to their great indignation – singled out for approval the recommendation on land purchase and expressed pleasure at the endorsement of his own request for the admission of 100,000 Jews to Palestine. Attlee decided to ask the United States forthwith to share in the military and financial responsibilities arising from the recommendations and to make clear to Washington that large-scale immigration must be ruled out until the illegal Jewish armed units had been eliminated. He added that the committee's recommendations must be considered as a whole. The American and British viewpoints seemed further apart than ever.

On 8 May, on the advice of Dean Acheson, who in Byrnes's absence at the Paris Peace Conference was Acting Secretary of State, the President sought a way out of the deadlock by proposing prompt consultations on the committee's report with Arabs and Jews. Attlee urged in reply that the military and financial aspects first needed study by experts of both governments and that the Arabs and Jews should be given a month, rather than the fortnight proposed by the President, to transmit their views. Finally memoranda of consultation were prepared on both sides of the Atlantic and submitted to the Arab Higher Committee, the Arab League, the Arab governments, the Jewish Agency and various Jewish organizations. The Arabs unanimously rejected the entire report and the Jews replied equivocally.

President Truman, as he says in his memoirs, realized that 'while there was much clamor in the United States that something be done, the country was neither disposed nor prepared to assume risks and obligations that might require us to use military force'. He had, in fact, asked his Joint Chiefs of Staff for their opinion and had been told by them that no American armed forces should be involved in carrying out the committee's recommendations; that no action should be taken that would cause repercussions in Palestine beyond the powers of British troops to control; and that nothing should be done to turn the Arabs away from the Western Powers and towards the Soviet camp.

48

The British Prime Minister now had the bit between his teeth and was determined that, if the United States wanted to press Zionist claims, she must be prepared to foot the bill. On 26 May 1946 Attlee cabled the President setting forth as many as forty-five points which had to be considered by the experts of the two governments before any decision on the report as a whole could be reached. Truman, though continuing to press for the immediate admission of 100,000 immigrants, on which Attlee not less stubbornly continued to stall, constituted a cabinet committee of the State, Treasury and War Departments, with alternates, to negotiate with the British. He made available the presidential plane to get the alternates to London, and they left on 10 July, under the chairmanship of Henry F. Grady, a former Assistant Secretary of State. They met with their British colleagues, headed by Herbert Morrison, against a background of increasing Zionist terrorism in Palestine. Attlee had decided that drastic action could no longer be postponed, and the High Commissioner had been authorized to clamp down on the illegal organizations and raid and occupy the Jewish Agency's headquarters in Jerusalem. Shortly after the American group arrived in London, the Irgun Zvai Leumi, the largest Jewish terrorist organization, blew up the King David Hotel in Jerusalem, which housed the main offices of the mandatory government and the British Army's General Headquarters. Forty-one Jews, Arabs and British were killed and forty-three injured. Three days later the Anglo-American experts, who had been working against time, had their plan ready. It called for 'provincial autonomy' – a Jewish and an Arab province in a federal Palestine. A strong federal government under the control of the mandatory government would have direct authority over Jerusalem, Bethlehem and the Negev and over such matters as defence, foreign affairs and immigration. The admission of the 100,000 was included, but made conditional on acceptance of the federal scheme. American economic aid was recommended for all the Arab states, with fifty million dollars specifically for the Palestine Arabs.

While Britain was completing arrangements for a conference

with Arab and Jewish representatives to consider this plan, the President cabled that he was not prepared to give formal support to it in its present form as a joint Anglo-American plan. Opposition to it in the United States was so intense, he added, that it was now clearly impossible to rally sufficient public opinion to enable the American government to give it effective support. He had instructed the United States embassy in London to press on the British government as an alternative a Jewish Agency plan for an independent Jewish state in part of Palestine. Attlee's reply to Truman was that, under the circumstances, any solution would have to be one which the British could enforce alone. The President's disavowal of his own appointees' recommendations led the Secretary of State, Byrnes, to wash his hands of the whole Palestine matter.

The London Conference, which opened on 10 September 1946, appeared doomed from the start. The Palestine Arabs boycotted it because the British had announced that the Grand Mufti (Haj Amin el Husseini) would not be allowed to attend and that they themselves would nominate the Palestine Arab delegates. The Jewish Agency, believing that it could rely on American support no matter how intransigent was its attitude, announced that it would take part in the discussions only when its own partition scheme was discussed, and refused to agree to the Labour government's decision to decide the composition of the Jewish delegation. So that not only the United States, but the two parties most closely concerned, were absent and only the governments of the Arab states and the British government took part in the talks, the Arab representatives insisting that they would not have met with the Zionists even if the latter had been present. They rejected the Morrison–Grady plan as a basis for discussion and called for an independent Arab State, to be established not later than 31 December 1948, with an elected assembly of which Jews could be members, but only to the extent of one third of the membership. Early in October, the British suspended the conference, stating that they required time to study the proposals.

An American election now loomed ahead which augured ill for any illusions the Arabs might still have entertained that President Roosevelt's declared intention not to allow Arab interests to be harmed would be honoured. In New York State, the Democratic Senators Mead and Lehmann were fighting a losing campaign for Governor and Senator. They told the President that a pro-Zionist statement was urgently necessary, for Thomas E. Dewey, Mead's opponent, was reported as being about to issue one himself. After some delay, owing to the White House not being satisfied with the State Department's draft, President Truman on 24 October issued one of the most disturbing statements on Palestine ever made public by a leading American figure.* It renewed his constant plea for the admission of 100,000 Jews to Palestine, omitted all mention of the Arab side of the case and also revealed that the President was prepared to recommend to Congress the liberalization of American immigration laws; and it emphasized most blatantly the way in which purely domestic concerns might influence American foreign policy. Many Jews even felt that the timing was singularly inappropriate – not only on the eve of election day, but on the eve of the Jewish Yom Kippur – and disliked as much as any an appeal to religious sentiment for obvious political ends.

The President's statement evoked an immediate hostile response from the Arabs, including a letter from King Ibn Saud alleging that the President had broken earlier American pledges, since his support of Zionism had led the Jews to extend their ambitions beyond the frontiers of Palestine, even to 'the confines of our Holy Lands'. In reply President Truman assured the monarch that responsible Jewish leaders did not 'contemplate a policy of aggression against the Arab countries adjacent to Palestine' and denied that his own policy in any sense represented action hostile to the Arab people. President Truman's statement also convinced the British once and for all that they could not rely on responsible American action in support of a just plan and made inevitable their

* Two days later Mr Dewey in fact called for the admission not of 100,000 Jews to Palestine, but of several hundreds of thousands.

precipitate withdrawal from the Palestine scene, with all its fateful consequences for the Palestine Arabs.

The London Conference was not resumed until early in 1947 so that the Twenty-second World Zionist Congress, which opened in Basle in December 1946, might consider the question of the attendance of a Jewish Agency delegation. The moderates, headed by Weizmann, Shertok and Stephen Wise, favoured participation in the London talks; but the activists, led by Ben Gurion and Silver, won the day and Weizmann was not re-elected president of the World Zionist Organization. Out of respect for his prestige and past services, however, the post was left vacant. The Arab Higher Committee was represented at the conference, its leading members having been released from internment. But there was still no United States representative, since Byrnes had agreed to send one only if both Jews and Arabs attended. Ernest Bevin played his last card. He submitted a modified version of the Morrison–Grady plan, on cantonal instead of provincial autonomy lines. In private talks with British Jews, he thought at one time that he had secured undertakings that would make a Palestine settlement possible; but the majority of the world Zionist movement seemed determined on a complete break with Britain. 'Policy,' Bevin declared bitterly, 'is being run from New York and how can I deal with American nationals?' The Arabs had continued to reject any form of partition. Exasperated and exhausted, Attlee and Bevin recommended to the British Cabinet that the whole problem should be referred to the United Nations and that, in any event, the British should withdraw from Palestine on 15 May 1948. The government was no longer prepared to sacrifice further British lives in maintaining unaided what had become an impossible situation.

To Dean Acheson, who had been in touch with Bevin's thinking during these months and was now Under-Secretary of State, the writing on the wall was clear: if the British were going to withdraw from leadership in the United Nations on Palestine as well as abdicate responsibility in the country, he did not see how the United States could safely avoid assuming some kind of leading role.

4. DANGEROUS ADVENTURE

On 2 April 1947 the British government asked Trygve Lie, first Secretary-General of the United Nations, 'to place the question of Palestine on the agenda of the General Assembly at its next regular session'. The British would submit to the Assembly an account of their administration of the League of Nations mandate and ask it to make recommendations, under Article 10 of the United Nations Charter, concerning the future government of Palestine. They further asked the Secretary-General to summon, as soon as possible, a special session of the Assembly 'for the purpose of constituting and instructing a special committee to prepare for the consideration, at the regular session of the Assembly, of the question'. What was to become, in Mr Lie's view, one of the most dramatic chapters of early United Nations history had opened.

The Secretary-General had been given advance information of British intentions, and procedures had already been discussed. He lost no time in setting in motion machinery for the first special session of the new world organization and on 28 April the representatives of fifty-five members gathered at

Flushing Meadow, the site of the 1939 New York World's Fair and – to the sardonic amusement of some diplomats – the temporary headquarters of the Assembly.

The United States from the first took a neutral stance; indeed, as Secretary of State, Marshall, pressed by twenty-nine pro-Zionist Congressmen for a statement of American policy on Palestine, had stated early in May that the United States government considered it 'premature . . . to develop its policy with regard to the substance of this question' in such a way as to limit the full utilization of the proposed committee of inquiry. In the General Assembly, Senator Warren Austin recommended that the committee's instructions be as broad as possible and, backed by the British delegate, successfully urged the exclusion from it of the five permanent members of the Security Council. They wished to make a record, he declared, 'That for all time, for all posterity, will be one of sound judgement and to make our beginning one that sets up as nearly an independent body as we can devise.' All other considerations aside, neither the United States nor Britain was anxious for the Soviet Union to obtain a foothold in the Middle East.

Although the special session had been summoned for a specific and limited purpose, it was soon clear that the dimensions of the whole Palestine conflict would be brought sharply into focus. Both the Arab Higher Committee and the Jewish Agency for Palestine had been allowed to appear before the Assembly's Political Committee. On behalf of the Palestine Arabs, Emil Ghoury declared that it was 'the determined and unequivocal will of the Arabs to refuse to consider any solution which even implies the loss of their sovereignty over any part of their country, or the diminution of such sovereignty in any form whatever'. The delegates of the five Arab members of the United Nations warned that any proposal other than the Arab plan for an independent, unitary state in Palestine would have to be enforced against the will of the Arabs of Palestine and of all the Arab states. Fadhil al-Jamali, the Foreign Minister of Iraq, cautioned the Assembly that 'supporting the national aspirations of the Jews means very clearly a declaration of war, and nothing less'. Speaking for the Jewish Agency for Palestine, David Ben Gurion declared:

> The great historic phenomenon of the Jewish return to Palestine is unique because the position of the Jewish people as a homeless people and yet attached with an unbreakable tenacity to its birthplace is unique. It is that phenomenon that has made the problem of Palestine an issue in international affairs, and no similar issue has ever arisen.

Sir Alexander Cadogan, Chief British delegate, put the assembly on notice that Britain 'should not have the sole responsibility for enforcing a solution which is not accepted by both parties and which we cannot reconcile with our conscience'. Mr Gromyko's declaration that the question of Jewish displaced persons was 'closely linked with the problem of Palestine and its future administration' caused a wave of excitement among the Jewish community in that country and in Zionist circles everywhere. Zionist enthusiasm mounted when, towards the close of the session, the Soviet substantive position was made known; the Russians endorsed 'the aspirations of the Jews to establish their own state'. The stage was thus set for the coming imbroglio.

The eleven-member United Nations Special Committee on Palestine (UNSCOP) was set up on 14 May. The countries represented on it had been chosen because none of them was considered to have any direct concern with the Palestine question.* The committee left promptly for Palestine and completed its work on 31 August. It recommended unanimously that the mandate should be terminated and independence granted at the earliest possible date; that the economic unity of Palestine should be preserved; that the sacred character of the Holy Places should be safeguarded and access to them assured; and that the General Assembly should immediately make an international arrangement for solving the urgent problem of the 250,000 displaced Jews in Europe.

* The countries represented were Australia, Canada, Czechoslovakia, Guatemala, India, Iran, Sweden, Uruguay, Peru, the Netherlands, Yugoslavia.

Another principle, adopted with two dissenting votes, stated that it was 'incontrovertible that any solution for Palestine cannot be considered as a solution for the Jewish problem in general'. A majority of eight members proposed the partition of Palestine into independent Arab and Jewish States and an International City of Jerusalem, to be administered under permanent United Nations trusteeship. All three entities would be bound together by economic union. A minority of three members, all with substantial Moslem populations, called for an independent federal government with Jerusalem as capital and for Arab and Jewish states having jurisdiction over such matters as education, social services, public health and agriculture.

When, towards the end of September 1947, representatives of member states of the United Nations converged on Lake Success for the second regular session of the General Assembly, an agreed American policy in the Middle East had not in fact been worked out. The view was generally held that it was desirable to have the backing of friendly Arab governments behind the United States defence perimeter, as defined in the Truman doctrine – Greece, Turkey, Iran; and that it was essential to ensure the smooth supply of oil from Saudi Arabia. But, at the same time, it was believed that America should lead the world in the humanitarian task of alleviating the lot of the remnant of European Jewry surviving the Nazi terror. Largely as a result of unremitting Zionist pressures, only the Zionist solution to this particular problem presented itself; thus there was not – and, in fact, there could not have been – a coherent American policy on the Middle East in general, or the Palestine question in particular. The representatives of various interests, and of various government departments, endeavoured to urge their individual Palestine policy lines on the President. In the midst of these conflicting ideas and pressures, Mr Truman had to determine national policy by himself. Unhesitatingly he decided that that policy should be to bring about, by peaceful means, the establishment of the promised Jewish homeland and easy access to it for the displaced Jews of Europe.

On 11 October, the Chief American delegate, Mr Herschel Johnson, acting on the President's instructions, rose to announce that the United States endorsed the basic principles of UNSCOP's unanimous recommendations and majority plan, 'which provides for partition and immigration'. However, he suggested certain amendments: for example, Jaffa, being an Arab city, should be in the Arab state, and all citizens, no matter where they resided, should have access to Palestine's ports and power and water facilities. He went on:

> The United States is willing to participate in a United Nations programme to assist the parties involved in a workable political settlement in Palestine. We refer to assistance through the United Nations in meeting economic and financial problems and the problem of internal law and order during the transition period. . . . In the final analysis, the problem of making any solution work rests with the people of Palestine.

Two days later, the chief Soviet delegate, Mr Semyon Tsarapkin, announced his government's support for the scheme. Until that dramatic day, the view had been widespread in political circles, and particularly in the Department of State, that the Soviet Union, with the aim of damaging Western interest in the Arab countries, would take a line opposed to the American one. The identity of American and Russian views on partition, at a time when the two powers were almost at each other's throats on every other world issue where their interests collided, seemed to most United Nations members and outside observers an event of extraordinary significance; it not only made the necessary two-thirds majority for partition a practical possibility for the first time, but also did much to restore the faith of many nations which, because of growing East–West tensions, had begun to fear that the new world organization would be totally ineffective in its attempt to solve international problems.*

* There is some doubt whether the Russian decision to support partition was, in fact, ever taken at top level; possibly this course of action was recommended by Foreign Ministry advisers (many of whom were Jewish) and approved by Stalin in a fit of absent-mindedness.

The UNSCOP majority plan had assumed that the British would stay on in Palestine for a transitional period of two years, to implement partition. An abrupt end to illusions on this score came when the Colonial Secretary, Arthur Creech Jones, told the Assembly that his government would only be prepared to implement a proposal acceptable to both Arabs and Jews and that they planned to withdraw their troops from Palestine by 1 August 1948. From then on the question of how to put into effect any plan which the Assembly might recommend became of crucial importance, particularly to the two super-powers. Britain, still the ruler of Palestine, held the key. No other country was apparently willing to make military forces available for the purpose. The United States had no intention of supporting an international force, on which the Soviets would probably insist on being represented; nor did she feel that American public opinion would agree to ask American soldiers to risk their lives in Palestine.

It took twenty-four days to exhaust the list of those wishing to speak in committee on the future government of Palestine. The Arab Higher Committee rejected both partition and a federal state. The Jewish Agency accepted UNSCOP's majority proposal as an 'indispensable minimum'.

On 21 October, the *Ad Hoc* Committee on the Palestinian Question (on which all member states were represented) set up three sub-committees. The first, composed of nine supporters of partition, was dominated by the United States and the Soviet Union; but a significant role was played by the chairman, Ksawery Pruszynski, a Polish prince with strong Zionist sympathies and an intimate knowledge of Palestine; and, at a later stage, by Lester Pearson, the future Prime Minister of Canada. The sub-committee dealt, among other matters, with two questions of crucial importance: the enforcement of the partition plan, and the frontier issue, of vital significance to the Zionists.

The second sub-committee, composed of the six Arab states, Pakistan, Afghanistan and – rather strangely – Colombia, was instructed to formulate a plan for a unitary Palestine state, along lines proposed by Iraq, Syria and Saudi

Arabia. A third sub-committee on conciliation reported eventually that there was little hope of conciliation; both parties were too confident about the success of their cause before the General Assembly. The UNSCOP minority proposal for a federal state thus fell entirely by the board, for lack of support.

The traditional borders of Zionism, from Dan to Beersheba – so appealing to the imagination of Lloyd George – had, with the growth of the National Home, gradually been superseded in Zionist minds by a wider geographical conception of Jewish statehood. The UNSCOP report had proposed that the entire Negev – the largest area of Palestine and the least populated, consisting almost entirely of arid wilderness – should be allotted to the Jewish state. The UNSCOP members had been motivated largely by their conviction that the Zionists would have the will, the ability and the pressing need to redeem the vast desolate region and uncover its mineral deposits and that, left to the Arabs, it would in all probability remain largely uninhabitable. The Zionists could claim that their urge to have the Negev also sprang from memories of the biblical past; in the days of Solomon and his successor kings, Elath, at the southern tip of Negev, was the only port of the kingdom of Judaea. No doubt what weighed more with the Jewish Agency delegation was the fact that Elath would give their state an outlet to the Red Sea and the Indian Ocean – essential to them in view of their strained relations with the Arabs, the existing Arab boycott and the possibility that they would be barred from the use of the Suez Canal. Elath was highly desirable, too, as a link with the Asian nations with whom the Zionists hoped to develop friendly relations and from whom they were separated geographically by a chain of Arab states.

Although sharp tussles broke out in the sub-committee over such matters as the frontiers of Samaria and the Dead Sea area and the location of Lydda Airport and the Jewish Holy City of Safed, the Negev formed the most important and controversial issue. The Soviet delegates were steadfast throughout in supporting the UNSCOP boundaries. But almost from the start the American representatives worked to restrict the area of the Negev to be given to the Jews, and in particular to assign Elath to the Arab state; by thus giving the Arabs a better deal, they hoped it might be easier to persuade certain uncommitted delegations to support partition. The American representatives were caught between President Truman's declared pro-partition policy and the doubts in the State Department itself and in other influential official circles as to the wisdom of that policy. Despite mutual suspicion and disagreements on various Middle East matters, America and Britain thought alike on Palestine partition frontiers, and particularly the Negev and Elath. If partition materialized, the British intended to support the incorporation of the Arab state into Trans-Jordan, as had been recommended by the Royal Commission ten years earlier. This would assure, through existing military arrangements between the two countries, Britain's access to the Suez Canal over its eastern approaches. The United States, worried about Soviet expansionist aims in the Near East and eager to limit her own commitments in the area so long as Britain could carry the ball, was ready to approve this line of action.

President Truman in his memoirs remarks that State Department officials dealing with Middle East affairs were, almost to a man, unfriendly to the idea of a Jewish state and that, to his regret, some of them were 'inclined to be antisemitic'. The pro-Arab sympathies of a few of them may have had as their background personal contacts with the Arab countries, sometimes through American cultural and missionary activities. But, as regards State Department policy, such factors were obviously of minimal importance. The United States in 1947 had committed itself to tackle fundamental military and political problems on a world-wide basis. American foreign policy was trying to halt the spread of Communism and Soviet influence by every means at its disposal. And, against this background, the question of Middle Eastern oil was of great significance. Tirelessly James Forrestal, who was, as American Secretary for Defense, deeply concerned over America's future oil supplies – not merely for possible use in war but also for peacetime needs –

warned of the danger that the Arabs, incensed by American support for a Jewish state, might deny the United States access to their oil. In this effort he was strongly supported by the State Department and the Pentagon.

An entry in Forrestal's diary for 9 October 1947, recording a statement to the Senate Committee on Small Business, reads:

I took the position that because of the rapid depletion of American oil reserves and an equally rapidly rising curve of consumption we would have to develop resources outside the country. The greatest field of untapped oil in the world is in the Middle East. . . . We should not be shipping a barrel of oil to Europe. From 1939 to 1946 world oil reserves . . . went up about 60 per cent while American discoveries added only about 6 per cent to ours. Until there were indications of new fields of substantial magnitude in the Western Hemisphere, I said, pipe for the Arabian pipeline should have precedence over pipe for similar projects in this country.

Forrestal, in his conviction that 'no question was more charged with danger to our security' than Palestine, also fought valiantly but unsuccessfully to lift the question out of American partisan domestic politics.

By the middle of November 1947 the General Assembly had finished its work on all the items of its long agenda except Palestine. Sub-Committee One was still bogged down, with the American delegation holding out on a number of issues, chiefly on the question of the Negev. The delegation's pressure on the Zionists mounted. It at one point decided that the boundary issue should be carried to the *Ad Hoc* Committee and the committee informed of the American reservations on this vital aspect of the partition plan.

For the Zionists, this was a highly dangerous strategem, not only because of the frontier issue itself but because their opponents could have exploited it as a pretext for confusing the entire question of partition. American hesitation on a major aspect of the plan might lead delegations otherwise ready to support partition to believe that there was no hope of securing a two-thirds majority when the vote came before the plenary session of the assembly. The fate of their state hung in balance; only the direct intervention of President Truman himself, they believed, could avert a calamity. On 17 November a call was put through from Dr Weizmann's hotel suite to the White House. Within an hour the reply came that the President would see Dr Weizmann on 19 November.

Mr Eliahu Elath, then a member of the Jewish Agency delegation and later first Ambassador of Israel to the United States, has described what transpired. Weizmann, he recounts, was at the time so frail that his doctors would not allow him to fly to Washington. But he was in an optimistic mood. The Jews had found, on an earlier historic occasion, a friend and sympathizer in Lord Balfour; now, in even more urgent circumstances, they would find a powerful champion in the President of the United States himself. And so it turned out. President Truman unhesitatingly promised that the American delegation would take a definite stand on all issues deriving from the declared position of the United States government on Palestine, and that no doubt should exist in the mind of any delegation of the American resolve to abide by this policy. 'We have to prove beyond all doubts that we are firm in our views and intentions,' Mr Truman declared. On the specific question of the Negev, he undertook personally to give clear instructions to the American delegation to press for the inclusion of Elath and the entire Negev in the proposed Jewish state.

At the very moment when this conversation was going on, the State Department was instructing the American delegation to inform the Zionists categorically that no support for the inclusion of Elath in the Jewish state would be forthcoming. A telephone call from the President came through to Mr Herschel Johnson as he was in the act of explaining this to the Jewish Agency delegation.

During the following two days the *Ad Hoc* Committee rejected first the unitary state proposal and then, by only one vote, a resolution denying the competency of the United Nations to enforce, or recommend the enforcement of, partition without the consent of the majority of the people of

Palestine. On 25 November, it adopted Sub-Committee One's partition proposal by a majority of only twelve votes. At the suggestion of the United States, responsibility for carrying out partition was transferred to the Security Council; a five-member United Nations Palestine Commission was to be established, to which, during the interim period when the two states were being set up, the mandatory power was expected progressively to hand over the administration of Palestine.

The Arabs, however, were still far from being defeated, though the role they were to play in the strange events of the ensuing days was largely a passive one. The Zionists faced the task of somehow securing the requisite two-thirds majority. Some observers felt that the American delegation, in their efforts to make clear to hesitant delegations the advantages of partition, lobbied with an energy more reminiscent of a national political campaign than of conventional diplomatic behaviour. But their methods were a model of propriety compared to those of the supporters of the Jewish Agency. The Zionists had their backs to the wall; but they were encouraged by most of the American press and buoyed up by the enthusiasm with which American Jewry had thrown itself into the fray. They launched themselves into a campaign so violent that it shocked even President Truman, sincere Zionist sympathizer though he was. In his memoirs the President recorded:

> The facts were that not only were there pressure movements around the United Nations unlike anything that had been there before, but that the White House, too, was subjected to a constant barrage. I do not think I ever had as much pressure and propaganda aimed at the White House as I had in this instance. The persistence of a few of the extreme Zionist leaders – actuated by political motives and engaging in political threats – disturbed and annoyed me. Some were even suggesting that we pressure sovereign nations into favourable votes in the General Assembly. . . .

Neither was the State Department immune. In his diaries, Forrestal records that Under-Secretary Robert Lovett observed at a Cabinet luncheon on 1 December, 1947 that he had never in his life been subjected to as much pressure as he had been in the three days preceding the partition vote. Herbert Bayard Swope and Robert Nathan (both of the White House staff) were among those who had importuned him. The Firestone Tire and Rubber Company reported that it had been telephoned and asked to transmit a message to its representative in Liberia directing him to bring pressure on the Liberian government to vote in favour of partition. The zeal and activity of the Jews had, in Lovett's view, almost resulted in the defeat of their objectives.

The pressure was applied indirectly and largely through American channels. Prominent in the campaign were Judge Joseph Proskauer, head of the non-Zionist American Jewish Committee, Robert Nathan, and the White House Assistant for Minority Affairs, David Niles. David Horowitz, then a member of the Jewish Agency delegation and later Governor of the Bank of Israel, has described the atmosphere in which his group worked at the time:

> The telephone rang madly. Cablegrams sped to all parts of the world. People were dragged from their beds at midnight and sent on peculiar errands. And wonder of it all, not an influential Jew, Zionist or non-Zionist, refused to give us his assistance at any time. Everyone pulled his weight, little or great, in the despairing effort to balance the scales to our favour.

Horowitz adds, 'The United States exerted the weight of its influence almost at the last hour, and the way the final vote turned out must be ascribed to this fact.'

Haiti, Liberia, the Philippines, China, Ethiopia and Greece became the objects of the most intense American pressure. Drew Pearson reported that Adolphe Berle, legal adviser to the Haitian government, telephoned to the President of Haiti to urge him to instruct his delegation to vote for partition. Bernard Baruch allegedly 'talked' with the French, who could not afford to lose aid under the interim Marshall Plan, and who switched at the last moment from abstention on the issue to a vote for partition. Eleanor Roosevelt worked untiringly among her many friends in the delegations and reportedly pleaded with President Truman to put pressure on the State Department. According to Forrestal, Loy Henderson said that Felix Frankfurter and Justice Murphy had both sent messages to the Philippines delegate urging his vote. A joint telegram from twenty-six pro-Zionist Senators, drafted by Senator Robert F. Wagner, was dispatched to thirteen delegations. It allegedly had the result of helping to persuade four governments to switch from negative votes to votes for partition and seven governments, who would otherwise have cast negative votes, to abstain.

To a group of representatives of national organizations, Dean Rusk, then Director of the State Department's Office of United Nations Affairs, admitted that certain unauthorized officials and private persons had violated propriety to exert pressure, with the result that partition was construed as an American plan by some countries and the decision robbed of whatever moral force it might otherwise have had. The American government as such, Rusk maintained, had never exerted pressure on member states of the United Nations.

The vote came in plenary session on 29 November. The partition plan was approved by thirty-three votes to thirteen, with ten abstentions. The public galleries, crammed to overflowing, were in an uproar. Rabbis wept openly for joy; and the representatives of the six Arab states swept out of the Assembly Hall.

From then on, the situation rapidly became chaotic. A prognostication by General Marshall that British withdrawal would be followed by a bloody struggle between Arabs and Jews was overtaken by events; the struggle began before the withdrawal had even commenced. On the day following the partition resolution, Arab attacks on Jews, with some loss of life, were reported in Haifa, Tel Aviv, Jaffa, Lydda, Jerusalem and on the roads. Further afield, riots broke out in Damascus, Aleppo, Beirut and Aden. Disorders continued to mount and when, early in January 1948, the members of the United Nations Palestine Commission, set up to take over the administration of Palestine from the British, assembled in New York, the Secretary-General endeavoured to hearten them by assuring them that they were entitled to be confident

> that in the event it should prove necessary, the Security Council will assume its full measure of responsibility in implementation of the Assembly resolution . . . the Security Council will not fail to exercise to the fullest, and without exception, every necessary power entrusted to it by the Charter in order to assist you in fulfilling your mission.

Even in those early days of optimistic trust in the efficacy of the United Nations, it sounded suspiciously like whistling in the dark; and Trygve Lie later confessed that he prodded the council so openly, not because he was confident that it would act, but because he feared it might not. There was no question of a great-power veto; but, as he put it, 'Other forces – Arab intransigence, British passiveness, American inconsistency, acted together to undermine the considered recommendation of the majority of the Member nations.'

Washington's enthusiasm for partition had, in fact, apparently begun to cool only a few days after the adoption of the 29 November resolution which it had done so much to bring about. Early in December, the State Department announced the discontinuance of the licence of arms shipments to the Middle East. As Britain was the chief provider of arms to the Arabs, this move worked to the detriment of the future Jewish state.

Mounting violence in the Middle East added weight to the warnings of Forrestal and others that American support of partition would do irreparable harm to her own vital interests. United States policy thus became uncertain just at the time when the Palestine Commission and the United Nations in general desperately needed forthright big-power support.

It rapidly became clear that partition could not be carried out by peaceful means alone. On 16 February, the Palestine Commission informed the Security Council that armed forces from surrounding Arab states had already begun to infiltrate into Palestine. A basic issue of international order was involved. 'A dangerous and tragic precedent will have been established if force, or the threat of the use of force, is to prove an effective deterrent to the will of the United Nations.' Unless an adequate non-Palestinian force were provided, the Commission warned,

> the period immediately following the termination of the Mandate will be a period of uncontrolled, widespread strife in Palestine, including Jerusalem. This would be a catastrophic conclusion to an era of international concern for the territory.

Many illusions were shattered when Ambassador Warren Austin, the American representative on the Security Council, addressed the council meeting summoned to consider the commission's report. The Security Council, Mr Austin contended, lacked the power to enforce partition or any other type of political settlement. America's contribution to the effort to deal with a situation rapidly getting completely out of hand was to suggest that the council's five permanent members – China, France, the Soviet Union, the United Kingdom and the United States – should look into 'the question of possible threats to international peace arising in connection with the Palestine situation'. In Trygve Lie's words, 'Washington had taken the heart out of any support which the Security Council might have mobilized to enforce peace and maintain the decision on partition.' The Secretary-General naturally looked at the whole matter not in the light of Arab or Zionist interests, but in that of the fundamental prejudice to the powers of the United Nations Organization and the possibly fatal damage to its prestige.

Of the five permanent members of the council, the Soviet Union alone stood firmly behind the partition recommendation. Rumours were abroad that the United States intended to abandon partition altogether. In effect, formal American repudiation of partition – or so it seemed to the world – came on the very day when a committee of the five permanent members reported to the Security Council on its recommendations for 'implementing' the assembly's plan. Mr Austin, acting on new instructions, took the floor to announce 'that the loss of life in the Holy Land must be brought to an immediate end. The maintenance of international peace is at stake.' He went on to explain that his country now believed that a temporary United Nations trusteeship for Palestine should be established. It would be 'without prejudice to the rights, claims and positions of the parties concerned or to the character of the eventual political settlement'. Pending the convening of a special session of the General Assembly during which the Security Council would recommend this trusteeship proposal, the United States believed that the Palestine Commission should be asked to suspend its efforts to implement the partition plan.

The American turnabout caused so much confusion that President Truman issued a statement declaring that it was vital that the American public should have a clear understanding of the position of the United States regarding partition. The government was not proposing trusteeship as a substitute for partition, he explained, but as an effort to fill the vacuum which would be created after the termination of the Mandate on 15 May. In his memoirs he went further; the United States had not rejected partition but rather had made 'an effort to postpone its effective date until proper conditions for the establishment of self-government in the two parts might be established'. Whatever the intention, the result was Arab jubilation, Zionist despair and the decision of the United Nations Secretary-General that he must resign – a step from which, however, the American and Soviet delegates succeeded in dissuading him.

The international mills went on grinding, and the second special session of the General Assembly duly opened on 16 April 1948 and debated for a month, in an atmosphere of almost total scepticism, as to the merits of trusteeship. It finally managed to adopt resolutions supporting the Security Council's efforts to bring about a truce in Palestine, appointing a mediator and relieving the Palestine Commission of the further exercise of its responsibilities. But it did not rescind its partition recommendation, which remained, and to this day remains, legally valid.

On the closing day of the special session, word arrived that, with the expiration of the Mandate, the Palestine Jews had proclaimed the existence of the State of Israel. Exactly eleven minutes after this news had reached President Truman, and at the very moment when the assembly was discussing a proposal put forward by the United States itself, jointly with France, for an international régime in Jerusalem, the President's press secretary issued a statement announcing that the United States had recognized 'the Provisional Government as the *de facto* authority of the new state of Israel'. The Security Council, when it met next morning, found a cable from the Egyptian Minister of Foreign Affairs informing it that 'Egyptian armed forces have started to enter Palestine to establish security and order'. The first shooting war which the world had seen since the end of the Second World War had begun. And the Palestine Arabs, thanks largely to American policies, were about to enter on their long ordeal of exile, dispossession and hardship.

At this stage the question can be asked: what was the practical impact of United States policy on Palestine, as so far described, on the native population of that country? Its effect was to deprive them of 66 per cent of their country in terms of area, 83 per cent in terms of cultivable land and 83 per cent in terms of industrial output; of their only port, Haifa, and their greatest treasure, Jerusalem, Holy City of Islam, Christianity and Judaism; of the little town of Bethlehem, especially venerated by Christians. This was, in fact, the position at the time when the United Nations, under extraordinary pressure from its wealthiest and most powerful member state, voted for the partition of Palestine into three separate entities.

5. THE PALESTINIANS

When President Truman decided in the autumn of 1947 that United States policy was to secure a Jewish state in a partitioned Palestine, the Arab inhabitants of that country numbered some 1,203,000. They represented two-thirds of the population, and had for the most part lived there for over a thousand years. Ninety-four per cent of the small country – Palestine is roughly the size of Wales – was owned or settled by them.* The other third of the population, the Jews, owned in 1947 only 6 per cent of the land. Eighty-six per cent of them had immigrated to Palestine since 1922.

Both the Arabs and Jews of Palestine were, in a sense, the wards of the United Nations. The new international organiza-

* The Palestine Arabs, however, were not the legal owners of 94 per cent of the land of Palestine. When the country was under Ottoman rule, all land belonged to the state and farmers were technically the tenants of the government, although they were allowed to buy, sell and inherit their real estate. During the British mandatory administration, most of the land was surveyed and registered in the names of private owners, but in 1948 when the mandate ended the process was not complete and some 3.4 per cent of the land was still unregistered. However, all unregistered government land was settled and in use by Arabs; the Jews did not buy land without registering it.

tion inherited responsibility from its predecessor for those territories which, since the First World War, had been administered as League Mandates, had not as yet attained independence and whose wellbeing and development had been defined in the League Covenant as 'a sacred trust of civilization'. This makes all the more shocking the fact that the United Nations, led by the United States, sanctioned in Palestine a state of affairs which amounted virtually to internationally legalized theft. In so doing, of course, it jeopardized its own moral authority in the post-war world, just as America, in espousing uncritically Israel's cause, undermined her prestige and good name in much of Africa and Asia.

For the Palestine Arabs, the injustice meted out to them in 1947 was, as we have seen, only a further instalment of the wrongs they had suffered from 1917 onwards. During the three decades Arab nationalism in the Middle East had matured and scored triumphs: Egypt and Iraq had been admitted to the League of Nations; they, and Syria and Lebanon, had become charter members of the United Nations; Arab Palestine alone, in culture and education considerably above the standards of many of the United Nations member states, was not yet free. The Palestinians naturally saw themselves as the only lawful inheritors of the Ottoman Empire; why should they be expected to allow an alien people to usurp their inheritance? Why had the Wilsonian principle of self-determination, universally accepted in 1918, never been applied to Arab Palestine? Why had they not been consulted on the terms of the Balfour Declaration? They had seen – and indeed had been all too well justified in seeing – in the proposed Jewish state only the threat of political and economic domination by the Zionists.

The Palestine Arabs are, for the most part, descended from an ancient people of the Near East, recognized in Hebrew mythology as close relatives of the Hebrews themselves and whose language, like Hebrew, belongs to the linguistic group known as 'Semitic'. They had not played any very notable part in the golden age of Islam between the seventh and tenth centuries, when the Arabs took the lead in world civilization and their trade and influence extended from Portugal to China. Only a few men of learning of any great celebrity were Palestinians. Jerusalem, in the seclusion of its stony hills, had, it is true, its university, but it could not compete with wealthier and less remote centres of learning; and the only masterpiece of art which has survived in Palestine from the seventh century is the magnificent mosque in Jerusalem known as the Dome of the Rock, in the centre of a wide stone platform on which the Jewish Temple once stood, and from which Moslems believe that Mohammed took flight on his magic horse to heaven. The Haram esh Sharif, or 'Noble Sanctuary', as the sacred platform is known, ranks with Mecca and Medina as one of the three great Holy Places of Islam.

By the eleventh century the Arab Empire had begun to disintegrate, and from then on Palestine was subjected to alien rule and for many centuries lay outside the main stream of the world's affairs. From the sixteenth century until the First World War it formed part of the Ottoman Empire, except for brief interruptions during Napoleon's invasion and Mohammed Ali's occupation. The Ottoman régime was lethargic and inefficient. So the Palestinians in 1914 might have been thought a 'backward' people. But then, as now, they were unwarlike, friendly, cheerful and industrious, deeply attached to the soil which they tilled and to the country – poor and neglected though it was – which was their home and had been the home of their ancestors for centuries past.

In 1948, about two-thirds of the Palestine Arabs were peasants. The adults were very largely illiterate, though highly intelligent. Nearly all the country people belonged to a small number of 'clans', the members of which were related to a common ancestor on their father's side. Every villager knew to which clan he belonged. Clan rights and duties were the subject of an elaborate set of traditional rules which had all the force of law as regards the village members but lay outside the enacted law of the land. All wrongdoing, even murder, was remedied by compensation and fine, and the conclusion of the affair was solemnized by a lavish meal offered by the culprit's clan. In all personal problems, villagers were accustomed to looking to older and influential persons in the village for guidance. In every village, persons could be found who knew the complete history of every parcel and plot of land belonging to the villagers, the names of the owners and even their respective shares – no mean achievement considering the great fragmentation of parcels of land in Palestine and the complexity of the system of rights to land inherited from the Ottoman régime. The villagers moved about very little; over 90 per cent were born in the villages in which they lived and the remainder nearly always came from neighbouring villages.

The rural Arab's family unit was his 'household' – traditionally all who ate bread made from dough kneaded in his house – and could include agricultural labourers and servants as well as a motley assembly of grandparents, sons-in-law, aunts by marriage, nephews and so forth.

The town-dwellers were, of course, far more sophisticated. Both Moslem and Christian Arabs (the latter numbered about 8 per cent of the population) benefited from the government's school system as well as from the multiplicity of educational institutions which had sprung up in the Holy Land, especially in and around Jerusalem. Though the politically minded suffered, as do most peoples who have lived long under 'colonial' régimes, from a tendency to blame others for unsatisfactory states of affairs, rather than to put their minds to remedying such conditions themselves, they were by no means without political organization. As the British mandate ended, there were seven Arab political parties in Palestine, three trade unions (one affiliated to the Jewish Histraduth) and three separate youth movements. The culturally relatively advanced townspeople were far more politically aware than the countryfolk; but the power of great landed families was still strong and a fascinating picture of an almost feudal society at the end of the Ottoman period and in the early years of the Mandate is given in Sir Geoffrey Furlonge's biography of Musa Alami, *Palestine is my Country*.

At this point it may be pertinent to ask how the Zionists themselves, before the United Nations partition recommendation, saw the problem of an Arab population in a Jewish state. Since 1937 they, or at any rate some of their more responsible leaders, had been seriously considering partition and they knew that no scheme would be internationally acceptable, given the pattern of land settlement, which would not leave a substantial Arab minority in a Jewish state. Alas, their public attitude was as devious on this as on the question of their true goal being a state, not a National Home.

The 1937 British Royal Commission, impressed with the success of Nansen's scheme (bitterly criticized at the time on humanitarian grounds) for large-scale exchanges of population between Greece and Turkey, had foreseen, and indeed urged, an exchange of population between the proposed Arab and Jewish states under its partition plan. In a revealing letter to his son, Ben Gurion commented in July 1937:

> We cannot and are not entitled to propose anything like this, because we have never wanted to dislodge the Arabs. But as Britain is giving part of the country which was promised to us to the Arabs for their state, it is only right that the Arabs in our state should be transferred to the Arab part.

In 1942, Weizmann had written that in the Jewish state there would be

> complete civil and political equality of rights for all citizens, without distinction of race and religion and, in addition, the Arabs will enjoy full autonomy in their own internal affairs. *But if any Arabs do not wish to remain in a Jewish state, every facility will be given them to transfer to one of the many and vast Arab countries* [author's italics].

The British Labour party's policy was invariably strongly pro-Zionist when the party was out of office and, as we have seen, only became unfavourable to Zionism during its relatively brief periods of governmental responsibility. In 1944 the report of the Party's National Executive pleaded that the Jews should be allowed to enter Palestine in such numbers as to become a majority. There had been, the report stated, a strong case for this before the War. There is an irresistible case now, after the unspeakable atrocities of the cold and calculated German Nazi plan to kill all Jews in Europe. Here, too, in Palestine surely is a case, on human grounds and to promote a stable settlement, for transfer of population. Let the Arabs be encouraged to move out, as the Jews move in. . . .

When word of this reached Palestine, there were excited comments by Jews and Arabs. Ben Gurion hastened to assert to a meeting of journalists that the Zionist programme for colonization was not bound up with any scheme of transfer of Arab population and that there was no need for it, although it was possible, of course, that Iraq and Syria would require, on political and economic grounds, an additional population and that they would be interested in encouraging a transfer of Arabs from Palestine. It remained, however, a fundamental Zionist policy that Jewish immigration and Jewish colonization must not be carried out at the expense of the Arabs.

As we have noted, bitter fighting broke out in Palestine almost as soon as the United Nations partition recommendation was announced. Some of the fighting was in the nature of guerrilla skirmishes; but it was at this juncture that the Zionists made one of their propaganda master-strokes. The world still believes that, in the 1948 war, the Arabs were the aggressors; this has presumably been the justification for Israel being allowed to keep territories won in 1948 through force of arms, in flagrant disregard of the United Nations Charter, and the grounds for the extraordinary fact that she was never censured by the United Nations for her seizure of 25 per cent more of Arab territory than had been allotted to her under the partition scheme. Incredible as it may seem, the governments of the United States and the other leading United Nations members turned a blind eye to the facts, though the record was perfectly clear. Before the end of the Mandate and the proclamation of the State of Israel in mid-May 1948, the army of the future state had attacked Arab areas outside her own United Nations borders. Thus the movements of Arab armed forces in May 1948 did not constitute aggression but were a reply to Israeli aggression. This Israeli action was not fortuitous: Menachem Beigin, Commander of the Irgun, has related that

In the months preceding the Arab invasion, we continued to make sallies into the Arab area. In the early days of 1948, we were explaining to our officers and men, however, that this was not enough. .... It was clear to us that even the most daring sallies carried out by partisan troops would never be able to decide the issue. Our hope lay in gaining control of territory. At the end of January 1948, at a meeting of the Command of the Irgun in which the planning section participated, we outlined four strategic objectives: (1) Jerusalem, (2) Jaffa, (3) the Lydda–Ramleh Plain, (4) the Triangle (the towns of Nablus, Jenin and Tulkarm), comprising the bulk of the non-desert area west of Jordan.

The first step in carrying out this plan came in April 1948, when Haganah attacked the 'International City of Jerusalem' with its population of 105,000 Arabs and 100,000 Jews, and specifically Katamon, a pleasant residential area chiefly inhabited by Arab families. From 25-8 April, Irgun launched an attack on the Arab city of Jaffa, allotted by the United Nations to the Arab state. They bombed it mercilessly for three days. On the fourth day the inhabitants panicked and fled, some as far as Trans-Jordan. They were the first Palestine Arab refugees.

Sir John Bagot Glubb, at the time British Commander of the Arab Legion (the army of Trans-Jordan) has described how, early in 1948, he interpreted at a private meeting in London between the Prime Minister of Jordan, Tawfik Pasha, and Britain's Foreign Secretary, Ernest Bevin. The Zionists, Tawfik Pasha said, had a government, a police force and an army ready to take control when the mandate ended; the Palestinians had nothing at all. As a result, several Palestinian deputations had asked King Abdullah of Trans-Jordan to allow his army to defend the area allotted to the Arab state – this to prevent the Jews from occupying the whole of Palestine, which they would certainly otherwise do, and in a matter of hours. Bevin replied, 'It seems the obvious thing for you to do, but do not invade the areas allotted by the United Nations to the Jews.' On this basis, Glubb relates, the Arab Legion crossed into the Arab area of Palestine on 15 May 1948. It never invaded Israel, in the sense of the United Nations 'Jewish state', but on the contrary, everywhere met Israeli forces invading the 'Arab state'. All the legion's battles with the Israelis took place on the territory of the Arab State or of the International City of Jerusalem, both of which had been invaded by the Israelis before the legion arrived.

In fact, except for the Egyptian army (some 10,000 men), which crossed from Sinai into the Negev, no Arab army attacked territory allotted to Israel by the partition plan. Lebanon took no part in the fighting; Syria fought one action at Samakel, at the southern end of the Sea of Galilee, and then withdrew. Iraq sent a token force of 3,000 men who engaged the Israelis across the River Jordan and then withdrew to join the Arab Legion in the defence of the Arab state in the Nablus–Jenin–Tulkarm Triangle. The 3,000 Iraqis remained on the defensive throughout. But the world has continued to believe that the Arabs, not the Israelis, were the aggressors (and moreover that a David–Goliath situation prevailed and that Israel faced an overwhelming Arab force – the contrary of the truth).* How else can one explain that after the six-day war in 1967, no voice was raised to suggest Israeli withdrawal to her United Nations frontiers of 1947, but only to her considerably larger pre-1967 area?

The exodus of the refugees, long considered an obscure episode, is now generally recognized for what it was. A deliberate master-plan had been evolved by the authorities of the future state to get rid of its Arab population – not through sober negotiations for exchanges of population, but in the chaos of war, and with savage dispatch. On 9 April 1948 the two main Jewish terrorist groups, the Irgun Zvai Leumi and

* Glubb, in *Peace in the Holy Land*, estimates the strength of the Israel Army at 62,500 and the combined forces of Egypt, Trans-Jordan and Iraq at 17,500.

the Stern Gang, attacked Deir Yassin, an Arab village west of Jerusalem, and deliberately massacred 254 women and children. News of this butchery rapidly spread among the horrified Palestinians and greatly facilitated the ruthless eviction which the Israeli army now proceeded to carry out in all sectors of the fighting. The result was that hundreds of thousands of hapless people lost their homes, their modest possessions and their livelihood. Their only fault was that they were not Jews; they did not fit into a Zionist state.

During this tumultous period in Palestine, American policy was chiefly concerned to spur on United Nations efforts to bring the fighting to a halt. The Security Council, with strong American backing, in fact called for two truces, the first from 11 June to 9 July 1948, and the United Nations mediator, the Swedish Count Folke Bernadotte, succeeded, not without difficulty, in persuading all parties to accept it, at any rate formally; for, despite the council's injunction that no war material should be introduced into the combatant countries, both sides spent the truce reorganizing and reinforcing their armies. In total the Arabs increased their forces to an estimated 45,000. But their only effective army, the Arab Legion, was actually reduced in strength from 5,000 to 4,000 and was severely handicapped by Britain's decision, brought about largely by American pressure, to withdraw its subsidy to the legion as well as most of the British officers serving with it. The legion was also short of ammunition and could not obtain rapid replenishments from British stocks in Egypt because of the United Nations blockade – as part of the truce measures – of Suez. Meanwhile military aircraft were smuggled out of the United States and Britain to Israel, small ships and coastal craft were acquired and a regular airlift was organized from Prague, bringing large quantities of small-arms, bombs, guns and ammunition.

In the ten days that followed the first truce, Israel forced back the Arab forces in the Central Sector, on the Syrian border and in Galilee. On 9 July she attacked Lydda and Ramleh a few hours after the ending of the truce. Loudspeaker vans drove through the streets ordering the inhabitants to leave within half an hour. Those who were reluctant to leave were forcibly ejected. The men were rounded up and driven away in trucks. Some 30,000 people, mostly women and children, many under fire from Israeli mortars, fled across open country in burning heat towards the nearest Arab village, ten miles away; many children and some women reportedly died during this pitiful exodus. The pattern of clearing out the civilian population from their homes was now clear. The inhabitants of the surrounding villages were similarly uprooted during the next days.

An Israeli attempt to push the Syrians from their positions on the upper Jordan River and round Lake Huleh was unsuccessful, but in Galilee they secured the plain of Zebulon, which ran parallel with the coast behind Acre, as well as Nazareth, and the Arab guerrilla leader, Fawzi el Kaukji, fled northwards. Cairo, Damascus and the port of Tyre, in the Lebanon, were bombed. The war was technically almost over.

At this point the Security Council, under United States leadership, ordered a second and, on paper, a far more draconian truce. Introducing his government's draft resolution, the American delegate, Dr Philip Jessup, declared that this truce was 'not to be considered an interlude in the fighting ... but is symbolic of the fact that the Security Council decides that the situation in Palestine is not to be settled by force, but is to be settled by peaceful means'. The new truce was to remain in force until 'a peaceful adjustment of the future situation of Palestine' was reached. The second truce entered into force uneasily on 18 July 1948. Both sides were left in no doubt that severe and rigid sanctions were intended should the cease-fire provisions not be observed. In Tel-Aviv, Dr James G. McDonald, a convinced Zionist, had been serving since June as United States representative to the Provisional Government of Israel – an appointment made by the President without the advice, or even knowledge, of his Secretary of State, General Marshall.* Dr McDonald told the Prime Minister, David Ben Gurion, that he personally felt confident

* He had been a member of the Anglo-American Committee of Inquiry on Palestine. He became America's first ambassador to Israel in 1949.

79

that President Truman would agree to American participation, should the United Nations decide to impose sanctions against Israel. Ben Gurion's retort was that, much as Israel desired American friendship, she could not yield on any point which would threaten her independence or security. Ominously, neither Israel nor the Arabs thought of the cease-fire as the end of the war.

Dr McDonald followed up this interview on 6 September, when he presented Israel's Foreign Minister, Sharett, with an *aide-mémoire* emphasizing that the United States was 'determined to use all of its influence to prevent a violation of the truce and – should unhappily such a violation occur – will support in the Security Council immediate action, if necessary under Article 7, against the aggressor. . . .' Additionally, however, the *aide-mémoire* sounded out the view of the Israel government 'in the strictest confidence' on such matters as a fresh approach to the status of Jerusalem; a possible exchange of that part of Western Galilee which Israel occupied as a result of the fighting for 'a large portion of the desert land in the Negev'; and finally, on the possibility of Israel considering some constructive measures for the alleviation of the distress of the Arab refugees, 'a factor influencing world opinion' (not, it will be noticed, a question of basic human rights).

The United States at this juncture was not convinced that peace could be obtained on Israel's terms and was unwilling to recognize her acquisition of areas outside the partition borders unless she made territorial compensation to the Arab State. Above all, the United States feared that Israel, flushed with military success, might resume the war in order to secure further gains. The question remained, if matters came to a crunch, how far America would be prepared to exercise her immense influence and prestige in Israel to curb her turbulent protégé.

Meanwhile Count Bernadotte worked desperately to demilitarize Jerusalem, to bring emergency relief to several hundred thousand destitute refugees and to complete the proposals for a permanent Palestine solution which he intended to submit to the United Nations General Assembly, due to open in Paris in September. He favoured a merger of Arab Palestine with Trans-Jordan; the inclusion in the Arab state of most of the Negev, Lydda and Ramleh; the incorporation of all Galilee into the Jewish state; the port of Haifa and the airport of Lydda to be free; and the placing of the Jerusalem area under international control. The Israelis had from the first disliked and distrusted Count Bernadotte as a mediator, believing that his sympathies during the Second World War had been pro-Nazi and that his views on the Negev and Jerusalem were British-inspired (earlier Bernadotte had advocated assigning Jerusalem to the Arab state). McDonald, in Tel-Aviv, felt that Bernadotte had blundered hopelessly; his proposals on Jerusalem were 'so offensive to the Israelis as to be incredible'; the mediator simply did not understand the significance of Jerusalem to the Jews. No doubt the United States representative was unaware that Ben Gurion himself had, only a few years earlier, proposed that Jerusalem should be left to the British to administer; but the Israelis themselves knew this and could not have forgotten, moreover, that only a few months earlier they had solemnly accepted the internationalization of the Holy City. The latest cause for Israeli resentment against Bernadotte was the news that the mediator intended to transfer his headquarters from the Island of Rhodes to Government House just outside Jerusalem. On 17 September, when driving from Government House to the centre of Jerusalem, Bernadotte with one of the French members of his staff, Colonel Sérot, was murdered by members of the Stern Gang. The criminals were never found or punished.

To two men goes the credit for alerting the conscience of the world to the desperate situation of the chief victims of the conflict – the Arab refugees, the bulk of the Arab inhabitants of Palestine – to Azzam Pasha, Secretary-General of the League of Arab States, and to Folke Bernadotte himself. It was, as Bernadotte recorded in his diary, Azzam Pasha who in Cairo, at the end of July 1948, called the mediator's attention to the deplorable conditions in which between 300,000 and 400,000 people were living. Bernadotte might, Azzam Pasha suggested, be able to start some humanitarian work on their behalf, or even try to make it possible for them to return to their homes. The plight of the refugees from Jaffa and Haifa was, he felt, particularly heart-rending.

In the report which he signed only the day before he was assassinated, Count Bernadotte included, with his territorial and other proposals, the following conclusion. It is his lasting memorial:

> The right of the Arab refugees to return to their homes in Jewish-controlled territory at the earliest possible date should be affirmed by the United Nations, and their re-patriation, resettlement and economic and social rehabilita-tion, and payment of adequate compensation for the property of those not choosing to return, should be super-vised and assisted by the United Nations conciliation com-mission. . . .'

And Bernadotte ended the section of his report dealing with the refugee problem by pointing out that large numbers of the Arab refugees were babies, children, pregnant women and nursing mothers. They were destitute, and were 'vulnerable groups' in the medical and social sense. As residents of Palestine, a former mandated territory for which the inter-national community had a continuing responsibility until a final settlement was reached, the refugees understandably looked to the United Nations for help. The mediator's own disaster-relief programme was quite inadequate to meet any continuing need; responsibility should be assumed by the United Nations, in conjunction with the neighbouring Arab states, the Provisional Government of Israel and voluntary organizations. Those refugees who returned to their homes were entitled to personal security, normal facilities for employ-ment and opportunities to develop within the community without racial, religious or social discrimination. The choice, Bernadotte concluded,

> is between saving the lives of many thousands of people now or permitting them to die. . . . I believe that for the international community to accept its share of responsibility

for the refugees of Palestine is one of the minimum conditions for the success of its efforts to bring peace to that
land.

The Government of Israel had already stated that fewer than
90,000 Arabs were left in Israel. Shortly thereafter, UNICEF's
representative in the Middle East estimated that the Arab
refugees totalled 500,000.

The scene now shifted to Paris, where the General Assembly
began discussing the mediator's posthumous report on 15
October; or rather, one of the scenes, for open warfare had
once again erupted in Palestine and a presidential election was
looming in the United States. On that same October day, Ben
Gurion, persuaded by his army leaders and against the advice
of his Foreign Minister, Sharett, launched 'Operation Ten
Plagues'. In defiance of the truce, the Israel Air Force heavily
attacked Egyptian airfields and bases. After about a week,
Egypt's northern front had been broken and her forces
pressed back. Only the Faluja pocket (where a young
lieutenant called Gamal Abdul Nasser happened to be one of
the defenders) held out heroically. On 28 October, Upper
Galilee was bombed. In three days, the Israelis cleared the
'Arab Liberation Army' under El Kaukji out of Galilee and,
in pursuing them, occupied a stretch of Lebanon. On 22
December, the final action of the war began. An effort on the
part of the Egyptians to relieve their isolated outpost at
Faluja gave rise to a fresh, and this time triumphant, Israeli
campaign, the sinister code name for which was '*Fait
Accompli*'. The Egyptians were pushed back into Sinai, the
Israelis close on their heels, only to retreat when Britain
threatened to intervene. On 7 January Egypt asked for an
armistice. The Arab-Israel War was over.

In the United States, the domestic political front showed
how remote were any chances of serious restraint being
exercised over Israel.

The platform for the Democratic party for the 1948 campaign had contained a statement on Israel which defined with
complete accuracy President Truman's own attitude on the

subject and had, moreover, been approved by the State Department:

> We approve the claims of the State of Israel to the boundaries set forth in the United Nations resolution of November 29 and consider that modification thereof should be made only if fully acceptable to the State of Israel.

However, at the opening of the General Assembly, General Marshall had announced, on 23 September, his government's acceptance of Bernadotte's recommendations as 'a generally fair basis for the settlement of the Palestine issues'. The Secretary of State urged the General Assembly and the countries directly concerned to 'accept them in their entirety as the best possible means of bringing peace to a distracted land'. He recognized that not everyone would be satisfied, but warned that unless the parties could accept this 'fair compromise', the debate could go on 'endlessly as in the past'. Back home this prompted an immediate accusation by American Zionists that United States policy on Palestine had once again been reversed, and some voices were even raised to maintain that the State Department had drafted the mediator's proposals. The President considered issuing a statement reaffirming the Democratic plank on Israel, but when Marshall returned in early October to report to the President on proceedings in Paris, he explained that his comment had merely been intended to encourage negotiations between the parties. When shortly thereafter news reached Truman that the British had introduced a draft resolution that he construed as in some way inimical to Israel's interests, he caused the following memorandum to be relayed to Paris:

> I request that no statement be made or no action be taken on the subject of Palestine by any member of our delegation in Paris without specific authority from me and clearing the text of any statement.

Truman recorded that he hoped to keep Palestine, and indeed all foreign policy, out of the 1948 election campaign. But the Republican candidate, Governor Dewey, made a public statement on Palestine which implied, or so Truman felt, that the President had reneged on the Democratic platform. This led Truman to make his celebrated statement of 28 October in Madison Square Garden, New York, a few days before his re-election, declaring that the subject of Israel must not be resolved as a matter of politics in a political campaign, but adding:

> It is my desire to help build in Palestine a strong, prosperous, free and democratic state. It must be large enough, free enough and strong enough to make its people self-supporting and secure.

The whole question of the area of the Jewish state was, the President's statement seemed to imply, up in the air; and in a letter to Weizmann, now first President of the State of Israel, on the anniversary of the United Nations partition resolution, he remarked that it did not take long

> for bitter and resourceful opponents to regroup their forces after they have been shattered. ... I understand very well your concern to prevent the undermining of your well-earned victories.

Truman possibly over-estimated the resourcefulness of the Arabs in comparing them to the Republican party, but he additionally told President Weizmann that he interpreted his re-election as a mandate from the American people to carry out the Democratic platform, including the plank on Israel. He was confident that the General Assembly would accept the United States's position that no changes should be made in the partition plan that were not acceptable to Israel. Recalling that the Export-Import Bank was actively considering a substantial long-term loan to Israel, he closed with the remarkable statement that 'what you have received at the hands of the world has been far less than was your due'. The pattern was set for one of the most unusual relationships between two sovereign states in history, though few could have foreseen that it would endure as American policy for nearly a quarter of a century, despite its harmfulness to United States interests and its disregard of all considerations of justice and humanity towards the Arab population of Palestine.

Meanwhile, in Paris, the General Assembly called for $29,500,000 in voluntary contributions (i.e. outside the regular United Nations budget) to provide relief for half a million refugees for nine months and asked the Secretary-General to appoint a Director for United Nations Relief for Palestine Refugees. An American was appointed to the post: Stanton Griffis, at the time the United States ambassador in Egypt. The Security Council had been overtaken by the speed of Israel's October blitzkrieg and did not adopt until 4 November a resolution calling for the immediate withdrawal to the pre-14 October position. It was disregarded by the Israelis, who had in any case had forces in the Negev before 14 October. On 16 November, the council called on the parties to seek the immediate establishment of an armistice.

The First (Political) Committee of the General Assembly had before it a long omnibus resolution proposed by Britain and based on the mediator's recommendations. Paragraph 10 of the original version of this draft resolution proposed that the refugees should be allowed to return to their homes at the earliest possible date, that adequate compensation should be paid for the property of those choosing not to return and for property which had been lost 'as a result of pillage, confiscation or of destruction'; and that the Conciliation Commission should facilitate the repatriation, resettlement and rehabilitation of the refugees and payment of compensation to them. What was contemplated was rehabilitation and compensation for refugees returning to their homes, as well as for those who chose not to return. The return home of the refugees was seen as an urgent and speedy way of solving a deplorable problem that had arisen as a result of the war and, moreover, one which could be solved forthwith, without waiting for the conclusion of armistices and peace treaties.

This, of course did not suit the Israelis' book; indeed they risked becoming prisoners of their own propaganda, for they had succeeded in giving the impression that the refugees had left of their own free will and in obscuring the fact that they had been brutally evicted from their bulldozed homes. Nor did they like the reference to pillaged and confiscated property. The United States came to their rescue with a draft according to which only refugees wishing to live in peace with their neighbours would be permitted to return home, and a choice would have to be made between repatriation and compensation. Thus the conditions under which the Palestinians might return to their homes were confused and obscured. The final text of the paragraph, which has been reaffirmed annually by the General Assembly and to which the refugees continued to pin their hopes for many years, reads:

The General Assembly . . .

11. *Resolves* that the refugees wishing to return to their homes and live at peace with their neighbours should be permitted to do so at the earliest practicable date, and that compensation should be paid for the property of those choosing not to return and for loss of or damage to property which, under principles of international law or in equity, should be made good by the Governments or authorities responsible.

6. MANOEUVRES
THAT MISFIRED

United States policy as the Middle East fighting drew to a close was basically to further the development of all resources in the area in order to raise living standards. The conviction – or illusion – was that, by this means, America could attain the two-fold aim of averting the threat of Communism from inside and of keeping the defensible countries – Greece and Turkey – on the perimeter of the region sufficiently strong for them to act as a bulwark against outside Soviet aggression. Britain was too weakened by the Second World War to continue to exercise full responsibility for the protection of the area: America felt that she had no option but to assume a leading role. A principal objective was Arab-Israel peace, and here the Government intended to work through the United Nations, on the basis, as Senator Warren Austin told the General Assembly, of Resolution 194 (III). It hoped to maintain friendship with both sides, as well as a military balance, and did not plan to supply arms to either party.

The drawback was that the Americans greatly over-estimated, then and for some years to come, the threat of Communism 'from inside' and failed to understand that the Arab world could not be roused by the battle-cry of resistance to Soviet domination and was intent only on obtaining justice in Palestine. President Truman's policy of 'Israel right or wrong' could not, in fact, be made to fit into the general pattern of American Middle East policy.

On the anniversary of the United Nations partition recommendation, Israel formally submitted an application for membership in the United Nations. Such applications have to go first to the Security Council, and there the United States strongly urged that Israel be admitted: but the application failed to secure the necessary seven votes. America, which desired peace in the Middle East as much as any country, did not seem to realize that Israel, firmly esconsed as victor and understandably self-confident though she was, might well yet have been prepared for the sake of United Nations membership to make concessions, and that, without such concessions on her part, there would be no peace. A valuable opportunity was thus missed.

Somewhat out of its depth in the uncongenial atmosphere of a minor blitzkrieg, the General Assembly had clung, in the autumn of 1948, to the mediator's proposal – which both the United States and Britain endorsed – for the establishment of a Palestine Conciliation Commission. The member countries felt that they could adjourn in mid-December, satisfied that they had been able to unload responsibility on to yet another Palestine Commission and one, moreover, on which America herself, together with France and Turkey, was represented. The new commission's formidable task was to bring about a peace settlement. As regards the Palestinians, it was charged with 'facilitating the repatriation, resettlement and social and economic rehabilitation of the refugees and the payment of compensation'.

The United States had scored one victory, though a negative one: it had succeeded in preventing Soviet Russian participation in the United Nations machinery for dealing with the Arab-Israeli conflict. Before the end of the British mandate, the Security Council had set up a Truce Commission, and the device was hit on of appointing to this body the consuls in beleaguered Jerusalem whose countries were members of the council – the United States, France and Belgium – the Soviet Union having at the time no consulate in the city. The pattern was set and the mediator in due course asked the same three governments to provide between them the 300 observers who, together with a few Swedish officers attached to Bernadotte's personal staff, made up the all-too-small Truce Supervision Organization. Nor was any Soviet citizen appointed to the staff of the new mediator, Dr Ralph Bunche, an American senior member of the United Nations Secretariat who had been one of Bernadotte's principal advisers, and who was now charged by the Security Council to bring the two sides together in armistice negotiations. He succeeded brilliantly, though it is doubtful if the Arab governments would have signed had it not been for the implied threat of renewed Israeli military action if they did not. The first agreement was signed on the Island of Rhodes by Israel and Egypt on 24 February 1949: those with Lebanon and Jordan followed in March and April. Syria, being in a state of more than usual turbulence from the end of March onwards owing to three successive *coups d'état* in nine months, did not sign until July. The Iraq government considered itself governed by the Israel-Jordan Agreement. The armistice agreements left Israel, whose population had amounted to 33 per cent of that of Palestine, with 80 per cent of the area of the country. The only part left to the Arabs was, ironically, the area held by Israel in Old Testament times.

America's consent to serve on the United Nations Conciliation Commission represented her first acceptance of direct responsibility in Palestine. The commission would, of course, have been greatly weakened had it not enjoyed American membership and, in fact, leadership. But the leadership seemed hesitant and, at times, incoherent. The United States had been injected brusquely into political responsibility in a complex region of the world and had to find its way on many different levels; delicate questions of adjusting relations with the British, the abatement of inter-Arab tensions, the need to gain the trust and friendship of Arab governments, the essential objective of Arab-Israeli peace. It was not extraordinary that a co-ordinated policy was difficult to attain. The Conciliation Commission itself was not helped by the fact that the American representatives, none of whom in the early years had much knowledge of Middle East problems or experience of diplomacy, replaced one another in rapid succession. They had hoped to get quick results and the stubborn difficulties in their path caused them to lose interest and give up the assignment on one excuse or another.

From its earliest days, the commission came up against the diametrically opposed approaches of the two parties to a settlement of the problem. The Arabs insisted that the refugee question should, because of humanitarian imperatives, take precedence over all other issues and that the only possible solution was one in accordance with paragraph 11 of Resolution 194 (III) (repatriation and compensation); the Israelis, who had no intention of allowing any but a minimal number of the Palestinians to return to their homes, took the line that the refugee issue could only be dealt with in the context of a general peace settlement: and they laid emphasis on the conditional clause under which only refugees willing to 'live in peace with their neighbours' could be allowed to return. Israel's Prime Minister, Ben Gurion, told the commission in Tel-Aviv that so long as the Arab states refused to make peace, Israel could not rely upon declarations that individual refugees might make concerning their peaceful intentions. 'The key to peace is not the solution of the refugee problem – the key to the refugee problem is peace,' he declared; the real solution lay in the resettlement of the bulk of the refugees in the Arab states. The commission itself, at any rate in its early days, was inclined to the view that the refugee problem was indeed bound up with other questions, and particularly that of frontiers; if peace talks were to break down on territorial issues, the repatriated refugees might once again be ousted from their homes. The American delegate, Mark Ethridge, however, pointed out to his fellow-commissioners that Israel could only accept a certain number of refugees; therefore the Arab governments should attempt to resettle the refugees by providing them with work, rather than relief, since there was not much hope for continued interim aid from the United States (by far the largest donor). No settlement of the refugee issue, he maintained, was possible except in the context of the general economic development of the Middle East.

At one time the commission seemed to be inching forward. The Arabs had accepted the principle of an international régime for the Jerusalem area and seemed ready to relax their extremely rigid position about priority of the refugee question over all other issues; the Israelis had at least declared that their government would be ready to take part in solving the refugee problem and would do this 'in a sincere spirit of co-operation'. Even the United States appeared to have retreated from its attitude of total permissiveness towards Israel. At the end of April 1949, at a moment when the commission had succeeded in getting both parties to Lausanne for peace talks, General John Hildring, a firm friend of the Zionists, arrived in Tel-Aviv with a message from Truman to Ben Gurion to the effect that the President was eager to maintain his friendship towards and aid to Israel, but was much embarrassed by her unyielding attitude on Jerusalem and the refugees. Despite this, a few days later, at the insistence of the United States, the United Nations General Assembly accepted Israel's renewed application for admission to the world organization, on the grounds that she was a 'peace-loving state' and that her government had given satisfactory assurances in respect of the implementation of the 1947 partition resolution and of resolution 194 (III) of 11 December 1948, and had 'unreservedly accepted the obligations of the United Nations Charter and undertaken to honour them from the day when it becomes a member'. The members of the Conciliation Commission were dumbfounded: not only had the 'peace-loving state' been engaged a few months earlier in acts of aggression in defiance of the Security Council's resolutions, but the United States had thrown away the commission's only trump card in its efforts to moderate Israel's intransigence – the one possible means of making progress towards a settlement along the lines prescribed by the General Assembly. To many Israelis, and notably to the Foreign Minister, Moshe Sharett, the question of United Nations acceptance and endorsement was of international significance and political importance; it set the seal on their international recognition. But to Ben Gurion, then Prime Minister, Israel had achieved statehood by her bold declaration of independence: 'The state is the result of our daring.' He never hid his contempt for the United Nations, and Israel's subsequent disregard of United Nations decisions has done much to lower the prestige of the world organization and reduce its efficacy.

The passage had not been a smooth one for Israel. As soon as the debate opened in the *Ad Hoc* Political Committee in New York on 3 May 1949, Senator Warren Austin of the United States delegation proposed that a vote on Israel's admission should be taken forthwith; but, in fact, the discussions took up ten long and arduous meetings. Israel was the defendant; against her were ranged, not only the Arab states, whose delegates, led by Dr Charles Malik of Lebanon, attained a higher and more statesmanlike level of debate than on many other United Nations Palestine occasions, before and since, but also several 'uncommitted' countries whose governments were obviously uneasy at the Conciliation Commission's reports of Israel's equivocal attitude on the refugee issue and of her outright refusal to accept an international régime for the city of Jerusalem; and outraged by the fact that Israel had still done nothing to apprehend and bring to justice the murderers of Count Bernadotte. Searching questions were put by the 'neutral' states: Belgium wanted to know whether Israel, if admitted to the United Nations, could agree subsequently to co-operate with the General Assembly in settling the questions of Jerusalem and the refugees, or whether she would invoke Article 2, paragraph 7, of the United Nations Charter (which deals with the domestic jurisdiction of member states). Denmark asked categorically whether Israel accepted or rejected paragraph 11 of Resolution 194 (III) and was curious to know whether she considered the rights of the refugees to their own property and their own country as rights of individuals or as a subject of negotiation between states; if the latter, how would the Government of Israel reconcile its attitude with Article 1, paragraph 2, of the Charter, dealing with the principle of equal rights and self-determination of peoples? Lebanon declared that, to admit Israel at that stage, would be tantamount to a virtual condemnation of one million Arabs to permanent exile; surely no delegation would endorse such action if it were aware of its implications. On behalf of Israel, Aubrey Eban fought a brilliant rearguard action; but the feeling of unease persisted and a Lebanese draft resolution proposing that the question of Israel's admission be postponed, though it was defeated by twenty-five votes (including those of the United States and the Soviet Union), received nineteen affirmative votes, while twelve states abstained. Britain, Denmark, Burma, Turkey and Brazil voted with the Arab states for postponement; France, Belgium and the Netherlands were among those who abstained. The United States delegate spoke only once and very briefly towards the end of the debate. 'The United States delegation,' Senator Warren Austin declared, 'together with the majority of the Security Council members, considers that the State of Israel meets Charter requirements.' And that was that.

Only a few days after Israel's admission, American policy appeared to have shifted once again. The United States ambassador McDonald called on the Prime Minister, Ben Gurion, to deliver a stern note from President Truman. The note expressed deep disappointment at the failure of the Israel delegation at Lausanne to make any of the desired concessions on refugees and boundaries; interpreted Israel's attitude as dangerous to peace and indicating disregard of the pertinent General Assembly resolutions; and reaffirmed that if Israel wished to keep areas seized in battle in excess of the United Nations partition plan, she should hand over equivalent areas to the Arabs as compensation. Finally, 'tangible refugee concessions' should now be offered as an essential preliminary to any prospect for a general settlement. The note contained an implied threat that the United States might reconsider its attitude towards Israel. McDonald records that Ben Gurion's 'off-the-record' response was: 'The United States is a powerful country; Israel is a small and weak one. We can be crushed, but we will not commit suicide.' As this unusual American envoy was leaving the premier's office, he said to Ben Gurion and Sharett, 'We have been through too many things together; there is no need for me to offer any comment.'

There was, indeed, no need, for Washington was again to back down. In its counter-reply to Israel's official response to the President's note, the State Department strongly emphasized America's 'friendly interest in the future welfare of Israel'. However, it did deny that immigration of Jews to Israel was a reason for holding up the return of Arab refugees and pointed out that Israel was trying to have it both ways – invoking the Partition Resolution when it suited her and denying its validity when it did not. The State Department was still, at that stage, taking its stand on the right of the refugees to return to their homes, as expressed in Resolution 194 (III). But, according to McDonald, the next few months marked a steady retreat from any position of firmness towards Israel on the part of the United States.

Since there was obviously no hope of firm United States action to break the deadlock, the Conciliation Commission turned its attention to the tragically urgent problem of the refugees. In August 1949, prompted by its American delegate at that time, Paul Porter, it sent to the Middle East an Economic Survey Mission, headed by Gordon Clapp of the United States,

> to examine the economic situation of the countries affected by the recent hostilities and to recommend an integrated program; . . . to facilitate the repatriation, resettlement and economic and social rehabilitation of the refugees and the payment of compensation . . .' in order to reintegrate the refugees into the economic life of the area on a self-sustaining basis within a minimum period of time. . . .

The Clapp Mission found that the Arab refugees numbered nearly 750,000 people. Their plight was 'the aftermath of a truce that was broken and an armistice from which a peace settlement has not emerged'. Tens of thousands, the mission reported, were in temporary camps, some in caves, the majority in towns and villages, sheltering in mosques, churches, schools and abandoned buildings. Their existence was an obstacle to peace in Palestine. The refugees had not been able to return to their homes because Israel would not admit them. They had not been able to earn a living in the countries where they had taken refuge because there was insufficient opportunity for them to do so. They had received no compensation for their property. United Nations funds so far subscribed to feed them would not last through the winter. The mission paid tribute to the governments of Egypt, Iraq, Jordan, Lebanon and Syria, who had provided help as best they could during the first few months of the refugees' exodus and had since contributed $6 million of the $32 million given by the United Nations for relief.

The mission found that the refugees themselves were the most serious economic dislocation created by the Arab-Israel war. They represented about 7 per cent of the population of the countries of refuge. Some 65 per cent had fled to the Gaza Strip and 'Arab' Palestine, almost doubling the combined population of these two areas. The remainder were in Trans-Jordan, Lebanon, Syria and Iraq. The great majority, the mission stressed, wished only to return to their homes. But since repatriation was blocked by Israel, resettlement outside Palestine a political issue and uncongested areas in the Arab world unavailable for settlement (unless much money and time were devoted to making them suitable for cultivation and development), the mission proposed that, rather than remain objects of charity, the refugees must be given work opportunities where they now found themselves. The only immediately possible constructive step seemed to be a programme of public works in the 'host countries', such as terracing, afforestation, road-building and so forth: such a programme would provide refugees with employment and at the same time improve productivity in the area. Rations issued by the United Nations should be reduced to 652,000 and should cease to be issued altogether after the end of 1950.

The result of the Clapp Mission's report was that the General Assembly at its Fourth Session established on 8 December 1949 the United Nations Relief and Works Agency for Palestine Refugees in the Near East (UNRWA) and gave the new agency the tasks of carrying out, in collaboration with local governments, the programmes recommended by the Economic Survey Mission; and of consulting with those governments on measures to be taken by them 'preparatory to the time when international assistance for relief and works projects was no longer available'.

The United States supported the establishment of UNRWA and assumed major responsibility for its financing. But it was already clear by the end of 1949 that she had departed from a Palestine refugee policy based, as she had assured the General Assembly only a few months previously, on the Resolution of 11 December 1948. For the look of the thing, she continued to pay lip-service to the principle of the right of the refugees, enshrined in that resolution, to an early return to their homes and to compensation 'under principles of international law or in equity' for abandoned, lost or damaged property: the United States had in fact voted year after year in General Assembly plenary sessions in favour of the reaffirmation of these principles. But she reserved all her influence and energies for a very different programme. The refugees could not return home; Israel did not wish it; they must somehow be resettled outside Palestine.

'Reintegration,' the American delegate told the Assembly in the autumn of 1950, 'will give an ever-increasing number of refugees the courage and material means of beginning a new life.' He hoped that the states of the Near East would weigh the advantages of such a proposal. The sooner the reintegration scheme started, the sooner would it be completed. Evidence would be needed of 'projects initiated' or to be initiated by local governments. The United States government, the American delegate explained, was ready to ask Congress for the necessary funds, but action would be influenced by contributions of other governments and preparations by the Arab governments for the reintegration of the refugees.

This was, of course, cloud-cuckoo-land. America had failed to understand the Arab world and its aspirations. She had apparently learned nothing from the experience of the British, who at one time had cherished the belief that the Arabs of Palestine would be reconciled to the Zionist presence in their country because of the increased prosperity which Jewish enterprise and ability would bring to it. Nor had the United States seemingly given much heed to the comments of the Economic Survey Mission, which had reported that the refugees believed that, 'as a matter of right and justice, they should be permitted to return to their homes, their farms and villages'. They were encouraged to believe this remedy open to them, the Clapp Report had continued,

because the General Assembly of the United Nations said so in its resolution of 11 December 1948. For purely psychological reasons, easily understandable, the refugees set great store by the assurance contained in this resolution. Most men in their position, given a choice between working in a foreign land or returning to their homes and to conditions understood and experienced from youth, would strain towards their homes, even were they told that, in their absence, conditions had so changed that they would never be happy there again. They would be reluctant to believe it. They would suspect a trap to hold them in exile until it was too late for them to return. Even if they were told their houses had been destroyed, they would still claim that the land remained. This seems a final argument to farm people.

In 1951, at Washington's suggestion, John D. Blandford took over the directorship of UNRWA, a post hitherto held by General Howard Kennedy, a Canadian. Blandford had wide experience of development programmes and had been general manager of the Tennessee Valley Authority; it was expected that he would set a reintegration movement on foot and give it momentum. In a joint report to the Sixth Session of the General Assembly, UNRWA and its Advisory Committee recommended a $250 million three-year programme, of which $200 million would be spent on 'refugee reintegration' and the rest set aside for relief. The General Assembly adopted this programme in January 1952. But already the following year the director had to report that the attitude of the refugees 'constituted a formidable obstacle to rehabilitation efforts': they would not, he said, accept anything less than a return to their homes. Soon the host governments were taking the stand that they were unable to approve actions which the refugees considered prejudicial to their rights. The $250 million programme never got off the ground. But the United States still stuck to its belief that, as the American delegate was to tell the General Assembly in 1954, the solution to the refugee problem lay 'in a new and stronger economy for the Arab countries and in the people of those countries coming to regard their refugee brothers as permanent members of the community and co-sharers in the Near East's future'.

The policy pattern on refugee matters was now set. We have seen what impact American policy had on the native Palestinians at the time when the United Nations, under extraordinary pressure from its wealthiest and most powerful member state, voted for the partition of Palestine. In 1947 a seemingly insoluble problem had presented itself. The United States at that time had to take some kind of decision in order to bring about a positive solution to the sorry mess bequeathed to the world community by Britain: the rough justice of partition was perhaps not much less unjust than any other solution. But in the ensuing years America could at the very least have exerted her influence to improve the lot of the native population by securing a fairer partition scheme. Under the sway of President Truman's enthusiasm for Zionism, she made no attempt to do this. On the contrary, from 1948 onwards, she deliberately engaged on a course which resulted in depriving almost the entire native population of their homes, their property, their livelihood, their nationality, their country and any effective voice on the international scene: meanwhile taking no action whatsoever to ensure that the victims received some kind of compensation, however inadequate, for these cruel deprivations.

99

There seemed an extraordinary gap between the level of governmental decisions and the actual effect of events on human beings. No doubt this was partly caused by the still strong emotional sympathy with the victims of Nazism, and by the bias in Israel's favour of information media in most countries of the world, so that the public, and particularly the generous and warm-hearted American public, never heard of, or imagined, the plight of the Palestinians and put no pressure on their government for real redress. In the flood of pathetic petitions, carefully inscribed in Arabic on cheap notepaper by the camp or community letter-writer, that poured into the office of the United Nations Secretary-General in the early days of the refugee exodus, there was no cry for revenge, no mention of sweeping the Israelis into the sea. The letters mostly told of deep anxiety about the little group of farm animals left behind: could the Secretary-General help, or at least tell the petitioner what he could do to make sure his animals were not suffering? When the first refugee fathers lined up in Jericho to receive food rations for their families, they were in tears because of the humiliation they felt at having to accept charity. The Palestinian country-folk who made up the bulk of the refugees in need had, for the most part, never before left their villages; that is what made their uprooting and exile such a traumatic experience for them.

All this was, of course, a side-issue to the main American objective of rallying the Middle East to the banner of an anti-Soviet crusade. Early in 1950, the United States turned down a request which Israel made for the purchase of arms in order to balance shipments being made by Britain to some of the Arab states under existing treaties. The United States, though as sympathetic as ever towards Israel, did not want to start an arms race. In May of that year, President Truman optimistically told Congress that:

In the Arab states and Israel, the fundamental requirement is a regional approach to the basic problem of economic development. This is urgently needed to reduce existing tensions, especially through the orderly settlement of homeless refugees. The programme for the Arab states will expand needed food production through the development of land and water resources. The programme for Israel will help that country to maintain her economy during an especially trying period of her national development. At the same time, the programme for assistance to the Arab refugees from Palestine ... has the threefold purpose of assisting the settlement of refugees, of strengthening those states wherein they settle, and assisting both Israel and the Arab states by removing this threat to the peace of the area. . . .

The President still had no conception of the bitterness of Arab feelings towards Israel; they wanted help to obtain justice in Palestine, not increased food production. Nor did he see that a policy of sweeping the refugee issue under the carpet with the broom of economic development was bound to increase rather than reduce tensions.

In any event, the United States was running out of ideas as to how actually to get the parties round a peace-conference table. In that same month of May, tripartite talks on various European problems were being held in London by the American Secretary of State, Acheson, the British Foreign Minister, Bevin and Robert Schumann, Foreign Minister of France, prior to a NATO Council meeting. During these discussions, the three statesmen also turned their attention to the troubled scene in the Middle East. Anti-British unrest and revolutionary ferment were mounting in Egypt and Iran; the Palestine Conciliation Commission's Lausanne talks had ended in total failure and the urgent and bitter problem of the Arab refugees seemed as far away as ever from an effective solution. In the hope of introducing some kind of stabilizing influence into the area, and of at least getting a chaotic situation within bounds, the United States, Britain and France on 25 May 1950 issued a declaration which, as Dean Acheson later observed, is not easy to explain. In it, the three governments recognized that the Arab states and

Israel all needed to maintain 'a certain level' of armed forces to assure their own security and legitimate self-defence and 'to permit them to play their part in the defence of the area as a whole'. All applications for arms and war material would be considered in the light of these principles. (The reference to joint Arab-Israel defence of the area was a first step towards the ill-fated Middle East Defence Organization; it was totally unrealistic since the two parties were still technically in a state of war with each other.) The Tripartite Declaration went on to point out that those states to whom arms had already been sold had all given assurances that they did not intend any act of aggression against any other state; similar assurances would be requested in the future from any other state in the area to whom the three governments might permit arms to be supplied. Should the three governments find that any of these states was preparing to violate frontiers or armistice lines, they would 'immediately take action, both within and outside the United Nations, to prevent such violation'. President Truman gave the Tripartite Declaration his approval and announced his belief that it would 'stimulate in the Arab states and in Israel increased confidence in future security'. Exactly a year earlier, America had solemnly warned Israel that territorial compensation must be made for areas taken in excess of the United Nations partition plan; in other words, she had refused at the time to recognize the *de facto* borders of Israel. Now the United States, as well as France and Britain, tacitly gave permanent approval to those borders and thus recognized Israel's title to land she had seized by force and in defiance of the United Nations Charter and the Security Council's resolutions. In other respects, however, the Tripartite Declaration had singularly little impact on the area of the kind that was intended, and the President's optimism proved to be ill-founded. Indeed, apart from providing the Arabs in general with one more grievance against America, and the Palestinians in particular with one more nail in the coffin of their hopes, the declaration was totally ineffective. Although it was to be repeatedly reaffirmed by both the Truman administration and the succeeding Eisenhower administration as the basis of the Arab-Israel policy of the United States, rarely had so large an undertaking, in Acheson's view, 'been so unlucky in its timing or had so shortlived an effect'. A few weeks later, the chief protagonist was deeply involved in the Korean War, and some months later all three governments were at variance with each other's views on the defence of Europe. And, as we shall see, when in 1956 one of the countries to whom the Tripartite Declaration applied did in fact violate frontiers and armistice lines, the three states which had issued the declaration were deeply divided among themselves.

It did not take the Arabs long to reject the Tripartite Declaration out of hand, on the grounds that it implied the recognition of Israel. They did not seem to heed the ultimate objective of the declaration – their association, with Israel, in the general defence of the region.

The United States was at this time obsessed with the threat of Soviet aggression. The Russians had perfected their atomic bomb; Eastern Europe and China had been lost to Communism. The Americans tended to treat Middle Eastern problems, including the Arab-Israeli conflict (whose importance they gravely underestimated), in terms of their own preoccupation with a possible East–West war. In their attempts to enlist the countries of the Middle East in their defence plans, they showed that they had completely misunderstood Arab priorities. The East–West conflict meant little or nothing to the Arabs. They discounted America's anti-Soviet propaganda. Although earlier they had been chiefly bent on ridding themselves of foreign occupiers, British or French, the factor now dominating their minds was Israeli aggression. They felt, in any case, that it would be less catastrophic to fall under Soviet sway than to be dominated by Israel.

The United States, however, pressed resolutely on with her plans for a Middle East Defence Organization. Turkey had just been admitted to NATO; it seemed an excellent idea that she should form a link between the two Western defence systems. On 13 October 1950 the United States formally invited Egypt and all other members of the Arab League to join MEDO; a similar invitation was extended to Israel. The proposal was, of course, condemned by the entire Arab world. In Cairo the Egyptian Prime Minister, Nahas Pasha, rejected it without even reading it. The Syrian Premier, Maaruf Dawalibi, spoke for all Arab League members when he declared:

> If speed is essential, an end must first be put to the aggression from which the Arab world has actually suffered before we need worry about repelling an aggression which is still remote and uncertain. Israeli aggression is an indisputable fact. If the alliance now offered to us is not to put a stop to Israeli aggression, what interest can it have for us?

For his Socialist opponent, Akram Hourani, the defence pact proposal was

> an imperialist scheme for the partition of the Middle East into spheres of influence. The British and Americans must choose between the friendship of the Arabs and the friendship of the Jews. The Russians are in any case not our enemies. Our enemies are the imperialist powers which occupy our countries and support Israel against us.

When shortly thereafter guidelines to the proposals were published by the sponsoring governments (the United States, the United Kingdom, France and Turkey), they elicited no response whatsoever from Middle Eastern countries, but roused on the other hand the Soviet Union to declare that the MEDO idea was 'directed towards the presence of foreign armed forces in the mentioned countries . . . [and] the possibility of continuous interference in the internal affairs of the Near and Middle East countries and the deprivation of their national independence'. The Soviet government could not 'pass by these new aggressive plans' in an area not far from its own frontiers. As we shall see, Russia's political strategy was to exploit the blunders of the United States and her allies in the Middle East and, above all, America's 'plain inability to appreciate the importance – indeed the total preeminence – of the Palestine grievance'. Here, in particular, Washington played into Moscow's hands. The Arabs had forgotten Russian sponsorship of the partition plan and her refusal in 1948 to countenance any suggestions for frontier adjustments – such as Bernadotte's – which might have made the plan more equitable and more acceptable to the Palestinians. The Soviet Union realized that the Western attitude, particularly towards the Palestine problem, would inevitably alienate the Arabs, who would then turn towards the Eastern bloc for support. Arab obsession with the Palestine conflict and indifference to the Cold War made it unnecessary for Russia to intervene to frustrate Western plans; all she had to do was to sit back and wait. She knew that a favourable opportunity would be bound to occur.

7. WHIRLPOOLS
ROUND SUEZ

Undeterred by her setbacks over MEDO and the chilly Arab reception of the Tripartite Declaration, the United States decided to use one country as a focus and centre of its Middle East defence system, its main preoccupation in the area. The choice fell on Egypt, which had in any case, under the MEDO scheme, been intended as the seat of the proposed Supreme Commander Middle East. When, in July 1952, revolution removed King Farouk and set up General Naguib as a front for the 'Colonels', led behind the scenes by Gamal Abdel Nasser, the United States was inclined to look optimistically on the new development; and Nasser's eventual emergence as leader of Egypt inspired hopes that here was perhaps an Arab personality of such strength and charisma that he would be able to surmount the seemingly impossible hurdle of concluding peace with Israel and carry his own country and the Arab world with him. Meanwhile, in September 1952, a representative of General Naguib had secretly informed the United States embassy in Cairo that the new régime might be ready to co-operate with America and undertake certain commitments, including participation in

MEDO, in return for military and economic aid. The Department of State was still trying to clarify the matter with the Egyptians, the Pentagon and the British when, in January 1953, the Truman administration came to an end and Dwight D. Eisenhower was sworn in as President.

There then entered on the Middle East scene a remarkable figure, John Foster Dulles – and literally entered, for he was the first American Secretary of State to visit the Middle East while in office. Dulles was the architect of United States foreign policy during Eisenhower's presidency. For an American president, Eisenhower was exceptionally reliant on his Secretary of State. He himself, wise, shrewd and prudent though he was, had little understanding or detailed knowledge of world history or international relations. He had to be painstakingly briefed on the elements of a new situation or problem. Dulles, supremely self-confident, a brilliant lawyer and negotiator, experienced, knowledgeable, forceful and, above all, full of moral fervour, was in his element in the task. Profoundly patriotic, he revered the office of president and liked and admired the endearing and world-famous man who filled it. It was a relationship of gratitude and admiration on each side.

The Republicans are traditionally less sensitive than the Democrats to Zionist pressures. Not long after he had assumed office, Dulles declared that:

United States policies should be impartial, so as to win not only the respect and regard of the Israeli but also of the Arab peoples. We shall seek such policies.

The occasion was a radio and television address to the nation, on his return from a twenty-one-day tour of the Middle East, India and Pakistan, during which he had been accompanied by a cortège of high United States officials, including Harold Stassen, Director of the Mutual Security Program. The United States, Dulles pointed out, should seek to allay the deep resentment against it that had resulted from the creation of Israel. 'Today the Arab peoples are afraid that the United States will back the new State of Israel in aggressive expansionism. . . .' Dulles had put his finger on the problem, but the solution escaped him. The Republican administration, he declared, stood fully behind the Tripartite Declaration:

> We cannot afford to be distrusted by millions who could be sturdy friends of freedom. They must not further swell the ranks of Communist dictators. . . .

Strangely, Dulles himself admitted in his address that the Tripartite Declaration had not sufficed to reassure the Arabs; and he was vague in the extreme about the problem of how Arab-Israeli peace was actually to be attained. All he said was that the United States would not hesitate to use its influence to promote a step-by-step reduction of tension in the area and the conclusion of ultimate peace.

As for the Palestinians, Dulles described the miserable conditions under which they were living. Some, he believed, could be settled in the area presently controlled by Israel; but most of them:

> Could be more readily integrated in the lives of the neighbouring Arab countries. This, however, awaits on irrigation projects, which will permit more soil to be cultivated. Throughout the area the cry is for water and irrigation. United Nations and other funds are available to help the refugees and Mr Stassen and I came back with the impression that they can well be spent in large part on a co-ordinated use of the rivers which run through the Arab countries and Israel.

They had not, however, come back with much understanding of the feelings and hopes of the refugees or with a full realization of the enduring hatred of the Arabs for the State of Israel. Indeed it was obvious to all, and especially to the Arabs, that the United States was primarily concerned not so much to bring about a just solution of the Arab-Israel conflict as to woo the Arabs to the cause of anti-Communism; and Israel, though she was bound to be adversely affected by this attempt to gain Arab friendship, realized that America would not try to diminish her commitment to the Zionist state's existence.

As President Eisenhower put it, with typical simplicity and straightforwardness: 'I don't know what I would have done had I been President when the question of Israel's independence came up ... but Israel is now a sovereign nation to which we have obligations. We shall keep them.' However, a request by Israel for a $75 million loan was turned down, and in October 1963 the United States temporarily withheld economic aid because of Israel's non-compliance with an order by the United Nations Truce Supervision Organization to halt work on a project to divert the waters of the River Jordan, pending consideration of the matter by the Security Council. The aid was stopped on 20 October but was resumed eight days later, Israel having by then ceased work on the project.

Meanwhile a kind of sub-war was developing along the border between Israel and Jordan. Many of the refugees who had fled eastwards in 1948 were living in camps on the hills of Judaea and Samaria. Other Palestinians lived in villages on, or close to, the demarcation lines. These people were not technically refugees, as they still lived in their own homes; but many of their villages were situated, as is frequent in Palestine, on high ground, separated by some distance, often several miles, from the village lands in the more fertile area below. The demarcation line, intended in any case as a temporary measure, had paid scant attention to this fact, so that many villagers found themselves cut off by the line from their fields and citrus groves – their only source of income – and even from their only water supply. An added source of bitterness was that, in their destitution and enforced idleness, they could watch from their windows strangers tilling their fields and harvesting their crops. Of those driven from their homes, nearly all had left behind them valuables: money, farm implements, animals, fruit trees, grain. Many from both groups – the acknowledged refugees and the 'economic refugees' as the frontier villagers came to be known – went back to their property at night to see what they could rescue. Those that were caught by the Israelis were shot. Later they went armed. The Jordanian government disapproved of these illicit border crossings by individuals; in 1954, half the men in West Jordan prisons were there on charges of infiltration into Israel. Glubb Pasha, who was responsible from 1948–56 for the security of the Jordan side of the demarcation line, has related that the government even suggested the formation of joint Israel–Jordan border patrols, a proposal which Israel turned down. 'Arab raids' were widely and exaggeratedly reported in the Western press and certainly helped to stimulate fund drives for Israel.

On 12 October 1953 Israel complained to the Israel–Jordan mixed Armistice Commission (part of the United Nations Truce Supervision machinery) that three infiltrators had thrown a bomb at a window of a house in an Israeli village, killing a woman and two children. Two nights later Israeli commandos entered the Arab village of Qibya, a mile and a half inside the Jordan armistice line. Every house in the village was blown up and sixty-five civilians, mostly women and children, were killed. United Nations military observers reached the village two hours after the Israelis left. They reported that:

> Bullet-riddled bodies near the doorways and multiple bullet hits on the doors of the demolished houses indicated that the inhabitants had been forced to remain inside until their homes were blown up over them . . . witnesses were uniform in describing their experience as a night of horror, during which Israeli soldiers moved about in their village blowing up buildings, firing into doorways and windows with automatic weapons and throwing hand grenades.

The United States, joined by the other signatory states of the Tripartite Declaration, France and Britain, took the issue to the Security Council: and Dulles, stressing that America had played 'an essential part in creating the State of Israel', admonished the Israelis that this was clearly an occasion 'to invoke the concept of decent respect for the opinion of mankind as represented by the United Nations'. The Security Council 'expressed the strongest censure'; and even such avowedly pro-Israel newspapers as the *New York Post* and the

National Jewish Post of Indianapolis compared the Qibya raid to Lidice.

But the refugees' clandestine border crossings, and Israel's savage acts of retaliation, continued. The paradox was that the people who carried out the retaliatory raids on poverty-stricken Arab hamlets, who subjected the Palestinians remaining in Israel to severe military rule and who behaved in general as ruthless conquerors, were living largely on American funds subscribed for humanitarian purposes. They were trying to have it both ways – to behave as proud victors and yet plead that they were a tiny country at the mercy of Arab hordes. They would have been in an increasingly awkward situation, had not Gamal Abdel Nasser come to their rescue. The wild threats broadcast over Radio Cairo about driving Israelis into the sea – made largely for domestic reasons, to encourage support of the masses for Nasser's régime – led the Western world to believe that a real threat of annihilation hung over Israel, and the flow of aid continued in full flood. With their consummate propaganda skill, the Israelis were wont to attribute Radio Cairo's utterances to 'the Arabs', inferring that a hundred million individuals had sworn to exterminate Israel. The threats came only from Cairo, with occasional outbursts from Damascus; and Israel, in Glubb Pasha's estimation, was twenty to thirty times stronger than Egypt and Jordan, the only countries with whom she had to reckon militarily.

To John Foster Dulles, 'colonialism' was second only in sinfulness to Communism and Americans in general felt that Britain was clinging too stubbornly to the anachronistic vestiges of her imperial power. Dulles continued to urge Britain to make substantial concessions to Egypt in the matter of troop withdrawals, his objective being the reconciliation of Egypt with the West. The British, however, looked on the Suez Canal – the route to Middle Eastern oil and to much of the Commonwealth – as a vital interest and were deeply reluctant to accept the abrogation of their 1936 treaty with Egypt and relinquish their canal base. Further, they had wanted to make the signing of a treaty with Egypt at least conditional on her entering the proposed regional defence pact. The United States preferred to take the chance that, once Egypt was fully independent of Britain, she would join the Western defence system of her own accord. The Anglo-Egyptian Treaty was eventually signed in October 1954. The Suez Canal Zone was to be evacuated by British forces, but Egypt allowed Britain to maintain bases in the zone and to reactivate them in the event of war against an Arab country or against Turkey.

Israel was alarmed by both the removal of the buffer between her and Egypt which British troops in the Canal Zone had represented and the fear that the treaty would result in Egypt joining the regional defence arrangement and Israel thus be excluded from it. She had even, when the treaty was still under negotiation, gone so far as to attempt to pass the *Bat Galim*, a vessel under the Israel flag, through the canal in defiance of Egypt's blockade of Israeli shipping. Israel's motive was, apparently, the hope that if Egypt impounded the vessel, the incident might be used by the many British opponents of the treaty as evidence that Egypt could not be trusted with physical control of the canal, thus enabling them to block the signing of the treaty. The manoeuvre failed completely: the ship was impounded, her crew imprisoned and the treaty was signed.

A little more than three months later, on the night of 28 February 1955, two platoons of Israeli paratroopers crossed the armistice demarcation line between Israel and the Egyptian-controlled Gaza Strip, attacked a military camp near Gaza railway station, completely demolished several buildings and killed fourteen Egyptian and Palestinian soldiers, an adult civilian and a little boy. Another group of Israelis ambushed a truck filled mostly with Palestinian soldiers coming to help to defend the camp. Altogether thirty-six soldiers and two civilians were killed, and twenty-nine soldiers and two civilians wounded. The raid was the most serious breach of the Israel–Egypt Armistice Agreement since its signature six years previously.

Early next morning, the Palestine refugees swarmed out of

their huts in the UNRWA camps, almost beside themselves in their misery and frustration that the Egyptians and the United Nations had allowed an attack to succeed on the one small section of the former mandated area that was still Palestine. Windows of UNRWA and Egyptian installations were smashed, cars and trucks burned and flags trampled on.

Why did Israel strike this sudden savage blow? Possibly as a demonstration of bravado, to counteract the feeling of intense insecurity then prevailing, because of the ever more violent hostility of the Arabs and the departure of the British from Egypt; or as retaliation for the hanging by Egypt of two members of an Israeli sabotage ring, who had been discovered in plans to bomb American installations in Cairo with the aim of poisoning relations between the United States and Egypt; or simply because Mr Ben Gurion – arch-proponent of the policy of severe retaliation – had returned from his self-imposed agricultural sojourn in the Negev desert to rejoin the government as Minister for Defence. But the Gaza raid, a minor affair in itself in terms of warfare, not only postponed indefinitely any hope of peace between Egypt and Israel but triggered off a chain of events, some of world importance, which inexorably led to a disastrous situation for the United States and her allies and even came near at one point to plunging humanity into a Third World War.

General Burns, the Canadian Chief of Staff of the United Nations Truce Supervision Organization, has recorded that Nasser told him that, after the shock of the raid, he could no longer maintain his policy of steering clear of trouble on Egypt's north-eastern frontier. Shortly before the raid, Nasser had visited Gaza and told his troops that there was no danger of war and that the armistice demarcation line was not going to be a battle-front; and, in the raid, many had been shot in their beds. Never again could he risk telling his troops that they could relax their vigilance. Nor could he enforce strict orders against the opening of fire on the Israeli patrols which marched along the demarcation line, only 100 metres or less from the Egyptian positions. Those positions were held by the friends, perhaps the brothers, of the men who had perished.

It must be remembered that Nasser, like all Egyptian officers of his generation, was still smarting under the bitter humiliation of Egypt's crushing defeat by Israel in 1948. This second demonstration of Egypt's weakness was not the only mortification that distressed and angered him in February 1955. That month Turkey and Iraq had signed a defence pact, in return for which they had received offers of military and economic aid from the United States. This was the first step towards a military alliance between the northern Middle East countries and Britain, which it was assumed that the United States would join and which had, in fact, been Dulles's brain-child. By June 1955, Britain, Iraq, Pakistan and Turkey were linked together and Dulles's 'northern tier' had become the Baghdad Pact; Iran was to join in October. The United States, however, to the consternation of the British, refused to join.* Nasser, in any case bitterly hostile to Iraq, whose Prime Minister, Nuri es Said, he feared as a potential leader of a rival form of Pan-Arabism to his own, was incensed that an Arab nation had joined the 'imperialists' and rightly considered that the Baghdad Pact would make it more difficult for him to carry out his own plans for the Arab world. The pact, if considered in conjunction with the Tripartite Declaration, confirmed that the Arabs were to receive arms for an East–West conflict, which they considered to be of no concern to them, but were forbidden to use those arms for the Arab–Israel conflict on their doorsteps. Apart from its disregard of Arab priorities, it perpetuated the very type of indirect Western influence which the Arabs most disliked. The United States could scarcely have found a more effective way of driving Egypt into the arms of the Soviet Union. And it seems almost incredible that Dulles should not have anticipated a Russian reaction to this new manifestation of the policy of containment on her very doorstep.

* In Eisenhower's view, it was not possible to join formally without simultaneously giving assurances to Israel, which in turn might drive Egypt out. However, the United States sent observers to certain pact meetings, and in due course became a member of its Economic and Counter-Subversion Committees.

Apparently unperturbed by such considerations, Dulles, addressing the Council on Foreign Relations in New York on 26 August 1955, enumerated the problems unsolved by the 1949 armistice agreements and which he saw as the main stumbling-blocks to Arab–Israel peace:

> The first is the tragic plight of the 900,000 refugees who formerly lived in the territory that is now occupied by Israel. The second is the pall of fear that hangs over the Arab and Israel people alike. The Arab countries fear that Israel will seek by violent means to expand at their expense. The Israelis fear that the Arabs will gradually marshall superior forces to be used to drive them into the sea, and they suffer from the economic measures now taken against them. The third is the lack of fixed permanent boundaries between Israel and its Arab neighbours.

Speaking with the President's concurrence, Dulles went on to reiterate the established American policy that the refugees should be resettled and, 'to such extent as is feasible', repatriated. But, he added:

> Compensation is due from Israel to the refugees. However, it may be that Israel cannot, unaided, now make adequate compensation. If so, there might be an international loan to enable Israel to pay the compensation which is due and which would enable many of the refugees to find for themselves a better way of life.
>
> President Eisenhower would recommend substantial participation by the United States in such a loan for such a purpose. ...

Fear could be overcome, Dulles suggested, by collective security measures guaranteeing present frontiers; hopefully, these measures would be sponsored by the United Nations. Thirdly, the United States would be willing to help to attain an adjustment of the armistice lines so that permanent boundaries could be drawn up.

This important, and, in many respects, generous and perceptive, speech was in the nature of a kite flown to test the reactions of the parties to the conflict. Unfortunately, it was singularly ill-timed. Dulles was speaking at a moment when the *fedayeen* campaign against Israel, based on the Gaza Strip, was at its height.* It consisted of guerrilla attacks against Israel, and mainly against its civilian population. Israel propaganda referred to the marauders as Egyptians; but the United Nations Truce Supervision Organization obtained evidence that, although the Egyptians organized the raids and trained and armed the guerrillas, the latter themselves were all Palestine refugees. The *fedayeen* campaign was, of course, Egypt's retaliatory move against Israel's Gaza raid; the Revolutionary Command Council were not sufficiently strong to launch any conventional military attack on Israel. In turn, the campaign was to serve as Israel's official pretext for her part in the tragic events of 1956. So it was not surprising that the reaction of both sides to Dulles's move was cool. The Israeli Foreign Minister, Sharett, declared that Israel would pay no compensation to the refugees until the Arab blockade was lifted, and that the value of property abandoned by Jewish refugees from Arab countries would have to be taken into consideration. As for frontiers, no unilateral concessions on Israel's part were even conceivable. There was no official Egyptian reaction, but the government organ *El Goumhouria* declared: 'Not a single Arab government would agree to discuss the proposals which are designed to serve no purpose other than the consolidation of Israel'; while *Al Difaa*, published in Arab Jerusalem, called the Dulles statement a departure from United Nations decisions and a new imperialist attempt to secure acceptance of Israel's existence.

The Baghdad Pact provided the Soviet Union with the opportunity for which it had been waiting. In the spring of 1955, the Soviet ambassador in Cairo, Daniel Semenovich Solod, began talks with Nasser on supplying Soviet technicians to Egypt, promoting trade between the two countries

* The Arabic word *fedayeen* means person ready to give his life for his companions; Arab broadcasts and newspapers usually translated it as 'commandos'.

and the possibility of Egypt's recognizing Communist China (at that time on friendly terms with the U.S.S.R.). At the Bandung Conference of 'non-aligned' nations in April 1955, Nasser, for the first time in his life, had met world figures and had scored a brilliant personal success. He came away convinced of the value to Egypt of Nehru's 'positive neutralism', but gave it his own special interpretation – that, in Dean Acheson's words, of attempting to play a male Cleopatra to the two superpowers. At the conference, Chou En-lai had pointed out to him that the Soviet Union might be a source of the weapons he so badly needed, not only to hit back at Israel, but also for an independent and activist policy. In May, Solod made Nasser a point-blank offer of arms. But it was not until the end of September that Nasser publicly confirmed its acceptance. The arms came *pro forma* from Czechoslovakia, they were to be paid for by barter and, most important of all, they came unconditionally. For the first time the Arabs felt genuinely free. It was the end of one era and the beginning of another.

The Soviet Union had vaulted effortlessly over the northern tier. All Dulles's endeavours to find a solid basis for peace and prosperity in the Middle East seemed to have come to nothing. He is said to have confided to a member of an American Jewish delegation that the Egyptian arms deal was the most serious development since Korea, if not since the Second World War. For his part, Eisenhower was convinced that, once the Soviet Union threatened to become actively involved in the Middle East, the United States had to step in to counter the weight of Soviet power. Although many factors were involved – oil, the Baghdad Pact, the supply of arms to Egypt – it is hard to see how the United States could have prevented the Soviet Union's entry into the Middle East unless she had been prepared to reverse her policy towards Israel and enforce a just solution of the Palestine problem.

Israel, in alarm at the Russian arms deal, applied in vain for arms to the United States. Her fears deepened when Dulles informed the Senate Foreign Relations Committee on 24 February 1956 that Israel, due to its much smaller size,

Could not win an arms race against Arabs having access to Soviet-bloc stocks. It would seem that Israel's security could be better assured, in the long run, through measures other than the acquisition of additional arms in circumstances which might exacerbate the situation.

These other measures, Dulles announced, included reliance on the United Nations, whose charter bound Israel and the Arab states, as members, not to threaten, or use, force; and measures which the three powers were going to discuss, according to a recent joint statement by President Eisenhower and the British Prime Minister, Anthony Eden, in the light of the Tripartite Declaration.

This must have seemed empty talk to Israel. A nail had already been hammered into the coffin of the Tripartite Declaration by the Russian arms deal, which had shattered the arms balance that the declaration was supposed to maintain; however, the French proceeded to redress the situation from Israel's point of view by selling her substantial quantities of weapons which matched at least in quality the arms Egypt was receiving from Czechoslovakia.

The project of helping to build the largest dam in the world at Aswan on the Nile had been before the United States government for some time. In November 1954, the United States had given money to Egypt for a further engineering survey. The International Bank for Reconstruction and Development (the World Bank) had begun a study that autumn of the Egyptian economy's ability to stand the strain of the project. Various American diplomats, experienced in the Middle East and abetted by the International Cooperation Administration and by other experts, now urged that the United States should try to offset the diplomatic and political reverse she had suffered in the Middle East by a dramatic gesture – help for the Aswan High Dam. It was, indeed, an amazing opportunity: an issue on which it might have been possible to win over most of the Arab Middle East. The High Dam was vital to Egypt, for her problem of increasing population and static resources seemed otherwise insoluble. It would not only make an additional two million acres available for cultivation, but would also increase thirty-fold the industrial potential of the Nile Valley. In December 1955, after discussing the matter with the British and French at a NATO conference, the United States and the United Kingdom assured Egypt of assistance in the financing of the dam, with the co-operation of the World Bank. The contribution of the United States was to be a grant of £56 million, followed by a loan of £130 million. The total cost, during fifteen years of construction, was estimated at £1,300 million. Protracted negotiations and investigations then ensued, as always when the World Bank contemplates a project of such magnitude (its share was a loan of $200 million). The American president of the bank, Eugene Black, himself came to Cairo for discussions with Nasser. While he was there, the rumour was abroad, and was widely believed in Egypt, that the Soviet Union had made a more favourable offer to build the dam. In fact the Russians had already offered help for the dam two months earlier, but the offer was in general terms and Nasser had not taken it up. But it so happened that the Soviet Foreign Minister, Dmitri Shepilov, who had in June 1955 attended the celebrations in Egypt of the British evacuation of their Suez base, made speeches in Beirut and Damascus on his way home in which he spoke of offers to aid Egyptian industry but did not mention the dam. This was interpreted in America and elsewhere as implying that the Russian offer was non-existent and Nasser engaged in a gigantic bluff. To Eisenhower, Nasser 'gave the impression of a man who was convinced that he could play off East against West by blackmailing both'. Dulles was outraged: he was to tell the Senate Foreign Relations Committee:

I do not believe in the U.S. being blackmailed, and at any time I sense a purpose on the part of any country to try to get money out of us by threatening that if we don't pay it money it will do something, at that point I say, 'Nothing doing'. . . .

Opposition in the United States to the idea of American

help for the High Dam was in fact building up steadily. The Zionists agitated against the *fedayeen* raids, complained that aid to Israel was taking second place and vigorously urged that the United States should not continue to let Nasser get away with blocking the Suez Canal to Israeli shipping. Southern Democrats feared that the dam would result in prejudicing the interests of American cotton growers. Congress was growing restless about the concept of foreign aid in general and had suggested that 80 per cent of American contributions for such assistance should be in the form of loans; and Dulles's Republican supporters were angry at Nasser's alignment, as they saw it, with Moscow. Dulles himself had begun to think that, because of the long and heavy burdens the construction of the dam would impose upon the people of Egypt, any nation associated with the project would eventually wind up very unpopular with the Egyptians. All these pressures were already making themselves felt when the loan was offered; but, to crown everything, Nasser on 18 May 1956 announced that Egypt had recognized Communist China. The Egyptian ambassador in Washington, Dr Ahmed Hussein, hurried home to warn Nasser of mounting American indignation at this move and to urge that the deal on the High Dam be clinched quickly.

The United States budget for 1956–7, announced on 4 July, contained the first appropriation for the Aswan High Dam. Early that month Nasser, who had in June been elected President of Egypt, sent Dr Hussein back to Washington with instructions to accept the American offer unconditionally. He was received by Dulles on 19 July, and told that the offer was withdrawn.

A unique opportunity had been lost, and lost in such a clumsy manner as publicly to humiliate Nasser, and hurt him where he was most vulnerable – his pride in Egypt. The State Department's official explanation only added insult to injury. The administration felt, it said, that, 'The ability of Egypt to devote adequate resources to assure the project has become more uncertain than at the time the offer was made.' The president of the World Bank, who had not been consulted, declared that it was the bank's responsibility to answer for the soundness of the project and for Egypt's ability to sustain it, and that he was satisfied on both issues. Later Black was to observe:

> It was the greatest disappointment of my professional life when the United States government saw fit to back out of that agreement in the heat of the moment. It was a classic case where long-term policy was sacrificed because of short-term problems and irritations.

But the contributions of the bank and of the United Kingdom were linked with that of the United States, and they, too, lapsed.

Nasser regarded the American slur on Egypt's credit as, above all, a deadly insult. 'When Washington sheds every decent principle on which foreign relations are based,' he exclaimed to an excited crowd at the opening ceremony of a new oil pipeline from Suez, 'and broadcasts the lie, snare and delusion that Egypt's economy is unsound, then I look them in the face and say "Drop dead of your fury, for you will never be able to dictate to Egypt!" ' Two days later, on 26 July 1956, he announced the nationalization of the Suez Canal. With the income from its tolls, he told a huge audience in Alexandria, Egypt would herself finance the cost of the Aswan Dam.

The unedifying drama which followed has been described in countless books and articles. No actor in it conducted himself entirely with credit. Of the leading participants, two were from the outset frankly bent on war: France – a permanent member of the United Nations Security Council and a signatory of the Tripartite Declaration – and Israel.

The seizure of the canal gave the French Socialist government under Premier Guy Mollet a pretext for an attempt to overthrow Nasser; if the Egyptian President remained in power, the Algerian War seemed likely to drag on endlessly.

Israel, as Ben Gurion told his Cabinet only the day before the invasion of Sinai, had two aims: the destruction and neutralization of *fedayeen* bases in Sinai and the Gaza Strip and, more vital, the lifting of the Egyptian blockade of the Gulf of Aqaba and the Red Sea. He added 'I do not know what will be the fate of Sinai. What we are primarily interested in is the coast round Eilat and the Gulf.' Above all, Ben Gurion saw that Israel had to take the tide at the flood; she might never again have the opportunity of attempting to gain her own ends, linked with two powerful allies. And the coming American presidential election may also have played its part in the Israeli Premier's plans.

Britain's position was more complex. When Marshal Bulganin and Mr Khrushchev visited England in April 1956, Eden had told them that Britain 'could not live without oil, and that we had no intention of being strangled to death'. Most of Western Europe's oil (and more than half Britain's) passed through the canal, which, to Eden's way of thinking, was an international asset and facility vital to the world. He considered it intolerable for Nasser to 'have his thumb on our windpipe'. In a telegram sent to President Eisenhower the day after the seizure of the canal, Eden stated that maximum political pressure ought first to be brought to bear on Egypt; but he added the clear warning: 'My colleagues and I believe we must be ready, in the last resort, to use force to bring Nasser to his senses.'

Additionally, Eden's rancour against Nasser was fed by Britain's loss of control over Jordan the previous March, as a result of agitation, directly inspired by Nasser, over the question of that country's adherence to the Baghdad Pact; and he also bitterly resented the acute difficulties Radio Cairo was deliberately creating for Britain in Iraq, the Arabian Gulf and Africa. All in all, the British government, like the French, was determined to make use of the Suez crisis to crush Nasser personally. The difference was that France cared not a fig for Arab, American, or, for that matter, world opinion, while Britain was beset by doubts, hesitations and confusion, fierce internal differences of opinion, and shame and embarrassment about collusion with Israel, to the point of direct governmental lying in Parliament on the matter.

As for the Soviet Union, on 31 July Khrushchev announced Russia's support for Nasser's action, which, he said, appeared to be completely legal. *Pravda* also declared that nationalization of the canal should be accepted by London, Paris and Washington.

United States policy was not simple or straightforward. On the one hand, the Western coalition could not but crumble unless America, Britain and France held firmly together, and Eisenhower in particular was unhappy about the rift with 'his right arm', Britain; on the other hand, not only Dulles but the great majority of Americans were emotionally opposed to 'colonialism' and, as Sherman Adams put it, sympathetic to the struggles which Egypt and other Arab states were making to free themselves from the political and economic control which the British felt they had to try to maintain in the Middle East in their own self-interest. The Americans felt that Britain was still living in the nineteenth century; and they rated Egypt's influence over other Arab countries very high. Above all, the kind of gun-boat diplomacy contemplated by her allies was totally repugnant to the United States, and especially to the devout pacifist that Eisenhower had become.

The Suez Canal was not of immense direct importance to the United States, except in so far as whoever held the canal was widely assumed to hold in his power the prosperity of many of her allies. America was able to bring herself to regard with equanimity what was totally unacceptable to Britain, Australia and New Zealand: control of the canal by Nasser's Egypt. The Western Alliance was thus split down the middle; and Dulles, to paper over the gap, proceeded to engage in a series of ingenuous and sometimes ambiguous, even devious, diplomatic moves, designed above all to prevent, or at the very least to delay, America's allies from launching themselves headlong on a course of violence. During a series of international visits and conferences, he came forward with remarkable assertions, some of which were astonishing and others of which were so vague as to be practically meaningless. On the first day of his hurried visit to London at Eisenhower's behest, for the purpose of persuading the British to review their plan to make war on Egypt, he told Eden, 'A way must be found to make Nasser disgorge what he is attempting to swallow!' At the London Conference convened by the United States, France and Britain to consider international 'operating arrangements' for the canal, Dulles declared that international confidence had been

> grievously assaulted. It is for us to consider whether that confidence can be repaired. If not, then we face a future of the utmost gravity, the possibilities of which we hesitate even to contemplate.

As Kennett Love has summed up:

> All the wordy activity of the ensuing three months, all the conferences, decisions, diplomatic missions and negotiations which seemed to the public and to many of the participants to be aimed honestly at settling a dispute over a canal were really a veiled struggle over whether Eden could make war against Nasser in spite of U.S. opposition.

If the United States was not candid with its allies, they in turn, though making clear their intention to fight, kept their actual military plans secret.

Meanwhile the Soviet Union continued to emphasize her unqualified support for Egypt. On 16 September the Soviet government issued a declaration stressing concern about the French and British military preparations. Russian arms shipments to Egypt were speeded up and large numbers of Russian and East European diplomats arrived in Cairo. A tumultuous welcome was given to the Russian pilots who took over on the canal from some Western pilots.

By mid-October, President Eisenhower was thoroughly alarmed and angered at the news of Israel's mobilization. He sent a personal message to Ben Gurion through the Israeli Ambassador, Abba Eban, who was returning to Tel-Aviv. Eisenhower later told Kennett Love that the message warned Ben Gurion that, if he entertained illusions that the American administration would feel it had to support Israel because of the coming presidential elections, he should know that Eisenhower's attitude was: 'First, I don't give a damn whether I'm re-elected, and secondly, we're going to do exactly what we've been saying [keep the peace], and that's that!' He forbade Dulles to translate this into diplomatic language.*

On 29 October the Israeli Army began to invade the Sinai Peninsula and the Gaza Strip, supplied, and with its airspace protected, by French aeroplanes.

The first casualties of the war were forty-seven Palestinian villagers living in Kafr Kassem, close to the Jordanian armistice line east of Tel-Aviv. That afternoon the Israeli Border Police informed the village *mukhtar* that an eleven hours' curfew would be imposed within half an hour and that anyone found out of doors would be shot. The headman told them it would be impossible to warn in time the villagers who were working in the fields or in neighbouring towns. As soon as the curfew started, the police forced returning men, women and children to dismount from bicycles, carts and trucks and machine-gunned them in batches. A sixteen-year-old girl was the only survivor of a truck carrying olive-pickers, all but two of them women, one of whom was eight months' pregnant. By six o'clock sixty bodies lay in the road, thirteen of whom survived by feigning death as the police walked about finishing off those who moved. As General Burns commented, the spirit of Deir Yassin was not dead among some of the Israeli armed forces.

The Israeli Army received the surrender of the Egyptian military governor of the Gaza Strip on 2 November. The Egyptians were still holding out at Khan Yunis, but gave up the following day. The Israeli troops then started a house-to-house search for *fedayeen* and arms during which hundreds of the inhabitants were killed and extensive looting by soldiers and Israeli settlers from across the border took place; the Palestinian inhabitants were unable to guard their property because of the curfew. Henry Labouisse, the American Director of UNRWA, reported to the General Assembly that the exact figure of civilian casualties was unknown, but that he had good reason to believe that 275 refugees had been killed.

* In the event, the President carried New York State by 1,600,000 votes; but the Republicans failed to win control of either house of Congress.

A week later, during an Israeli round-up for intelligence screening at UNRWA's large Rafah Camp, over 100 persons were killed when the soldiers for an undetermined reason fired on the assembled refugees.

On 30 October, an Anglo-French ultimatum was delivered (as already agreed secretly with Israel), feigning to be a peace manoeuvre. It called on Egypt and Israel to withdraw to a distance of sixteen kilometres from each bank of the canal. The next day the Anglo-French invasion of Egypt took place. On 1 November the United Nations General Assembly, at United States' prompting, urged an immediate cease-fire and withdrawal. Meanwhile President Eisenhower in a radio and television address to the nation declared:

> ... The actions taken can scarcely be reconciled with the principles and purposes of the United Nations to which we have all subscribed. And beyond this, we are forced to doubt even if resort to war will for long serve the permanent interest of the attacking nations. ... There can be no peace without law. And there can be no law if we were to invoke one code of international conduct for those who oppose us and another for our friends.

It was not until 4 November that the Russians, who had been fully occupied with the Hungarian revolt, joined in. The Foreign Minister, Shepilov, wrote to the President of the Security Council declaring the Soviet Union's readiness to send 'the air and naval forces necessary to defend Egypt' and Bulganin proposed to Eisenhower 'joint and immediate use of the forces of both powers to end the attack' – an offer summarily rejected by the White House. The following day British and French paratroops were dropped in the Canal Zone. That night a letter from Bulganin reached Eden warning him that the conflict could grow into a Third World War. The Soviet Premier also wrote to Mollet that Russia was 'fully determined to use force in order to smash the aggressors and restore peace in the East'. But Bulganin's most menacing letter was to Israel, which, he said, was 'criminally and irresponsibly playing with the fate of peace' and had put in jeopardy her very existence as a state.

On 6 November, Eden gave in, moved not so much by the Russian menaces as by a disastrous run on sterling, largely in American markets. Mollet reluctantly followed suit. Next day a jubilant Ben Gurion told the Knessett, 'We have created the third Kingdom of Israel!'

Britain and France evacuated Egypt by 22 December 1956 and Israel left Sinai a month later, making way for the newly formed United Nations Emergency Force which was on its way to take up its headquarters in Gaza. But Ben Gurion, with what Eden described in his memoirs as 'brilliant courage', still defied Eisenhower's unremitting pressure on him to withdraw from the Gaza Strip and Sharm al-Sheikh on the Straits of Tiran, the key point of his whole campaign. By mid-February, Dulles was contending that the United States had reached the limit in efforts to make it easy for Israel to withdraw. Anything more would endanger Western influence by convincing the Arabs that United States policy was controlled by American Zionists and that their only hope, therefore, lay in a firm association with the Soviet Union. Dulles, George Humphrey, the Secretary of the Treasury, and Henry Cabot Lodge, the United States Representative to the United Nations, decided with Eisenhower that 'the White House had to make a stand against Congress and against Israel'. Meanwhile a large majority had built up in the United Nations for sanctions and a resolution had been introduced by a group of Arab and Asian countries demanding the end of all aid to Israel if she did not complete her withdrawal. Ben Gurion capitulated in time to prevent the resolution from being brought to a vote. The Israelis left Gaza on 7 March and returned on 16 March to Israel from Sharm al-Sheikh, where UNEF troops were, it was agreed, to be stationed until permanent arrangements for freedom of navigation could be secured. Ten years of relative quiet in the Arab-Israel conflict began, between the wars.

8. AGGRESSION AND ITS CONSEQUENCES

I

Ironically, the Suez War achieved the very opposite of what two of its protagonists – France and Britain – had chiefly aimed for: Nasser was not overthrown, and on the contrary emerged not only as the hero and accepted leader of the greater part of the Arab world, and most particularly of the bulk of the Arab refugees, but as a dominant figure on the world stage. Of the three Suez partners, Israel alone managed to secure her two main war aims; for the stationing of the United Nations Emergency Force in the Gaza Strip all but eliminated *fedayeen* raids into Israel from that area and its presence at Sharm al-Sheikh meant that ships carrying goods to or from Israel would henceforth be able to make unhindered use of the port of Elath. Furthermore, Israel's military prestige had been dramatically enhanced. But the gap between her and the Arab world had widened dangerously.

On 5 January 1957, in a special address to Congress, President Eisenhower declared that, though the evolution to independence in the Middle East had in the main been a peaceful process,

> the area has often been troubled. Persistent cross-currents of distrust and fear with raids back and forth across national boundaries have brought about a high degree of instability in the Middle East . . . the relatively large attack by Israel in October has intensified the basic differences between that nation and its Arab neighbours. All this instability has been heightened and, at times, manipulated by international Communism.

The reason for Russia's interest in the area was, the President stated,

> Solely that of power politics. Considering her announced purpose of communizing the world, it is easy to understand her hopes of dominating the Middle East.

It followed, therefore, that a greater responsibility now devolved upon the United States 'to make more evident its willingness to support the independence of the freedom-loving nations of the area'. To this end, America should be ready to oppose, if need be by force, any Communist aggression in the area and to devote $200 million over two years to massive aid designed to strengthen anti-Communist elements. The President would seek for this purpose the authorization of Congress to negotiate economic aid programmes as well as military aid, including the use of United States armed forces, to protect the territorial integrity and political independence of nations or groups of nations seeking such aid 'against overt armed aggression from any nation controlled by international Communism'.

The Eisenhower Doctrine had been evolved during the Suez crisis and had been one of the reasons for Dulles's determination, despite powerful Senate opposition, to support United Nations demands that Israel withdraw from territory occupied during that war; he wished to ensure a sympathetic climate in the Arab world in which to launch the new policy. Washington believed that this policy would be universally acclaimed. The Baghdad Pact countries would feel that their cause had been strengthened almost as effectively as if America had actually joined the pact; on the other hand, critics and enemies of the pact, in the Arab world and elsewhere, would derive comfort from the fact that she had not joined. Israel would greet with alacrity the new token of American involvement in the area and the fact that it would cover her own independence and integrity. America's allies in Europe would, it was expected, welcome a firm lead from her, while at home Americans themselves would rejoice that no wholesale doling out of assistance was contemplated; only countries dedicated to combating Communism would be eligible for help. For his part, Dulles was sure that aid dispensed under the Eisenhower Doctrine must be unilateral; nothing, in his view, was more likely to encourage the growth of Communism in the Middle East 'than for us to go there hand in hand with the British and the French'.

There was no unanimous enthusiasm in the Congress for the Eisenhower Doctrine. Many realized, as did Senator John F. Kennedy, that it 'treated the Middle East as an American province to be defended against external aggression when, in fact, the indigenous Arab nationalist revolution and internal Communist subversion were the crucial factors'. But there was no question of repudiating the President's policy, for this would have been an open invitation to Russia to disregard America's warnings. Congress adopted the doctrine on 9 March 1957.

It was clear that the United States was seeking to fill what it considered to be a dangerous power vacuum caused by the progressive weakening of France and Britain and their elimination as political forces in the area as a result of the Suez War. In both countries, even those who had opposed the war were indignant that their long national history of concern and friendship for the Arab world should be entirely blotted out by what they saw as a temporary, though disastrous, error. Unhappily, the American press centred its attention on the 'vacuum' aspect, thus succeeding in wiping out in advance the advantages Washington had hoped to derive in the Middle

East from its new policy. The Arab reaction was predictable. Not only did the familiar cry go up that if the United States desired good relations with the Arab world, it must forget the anti-Communist crusade and turn its attention to the Arab confrontation with Israel, but Arab pride was hurt by the deeply humiliating 'vacuum' theory. In Syria, the Foreign Minister, Mr Bitar, declared that the Eisenhower Doctrine was one and the same thing as the Baghdad Pact. (It was at this juncture that Syria turned to the Soviet Union and began to receive economic and, above all, military aid on a generous scale.) As for the Russians, though they condemned the doctrine as an American attempt to take over former French and British responsibilities on behalf of American military domination, they must have been laughing up their sleeves, for the immediate result of the Eisenhower Doctrine was to increase their own prestige in the Arab world. They countered swiftly by suggesting that a four-power declaration be issued on the Middle East. This idea met with no favour in the United States, France or Britain, for none of the three wished formally to recognize the Russian stake in the area. For his part, President Nasser, entrenched in his position as a leader of a non-aligned nation, made it clear that he wished to have no truck with either the Eisenhower Doctrine or the Russian proposal, while at the same time stressing that the Soviet Union, unlike the United States, had given unremitting support to Egypt.

Nevertheless, the Eisenhower Doctrine scored some initial successes. It was backed by Saudi Arabia and formally adhered to by Lebanon, Turkey, Iran and Iraq. Jordan, torn by internal strife and feeling unable to adhere, gave its 'assent'. But the chief result of the doctrine was a great upsurge of Arab solidarity, championed by Nasser.

The decade which followed the announcement of the Eisenhower Doctrine and the Israeli evacuation of the Gaza Strip and Sharm al-Sheikh – induced only by months of unremitting pressure by the President – was full of drama and tumult in the Middle East. Egypt and Syria joined together to form the United Arab Republic, only to see it dissolve less than four years later, when the Syrian government, following an internal *coup d'état*, withdrew from the union; revolution destroyed the Hashemite monarchy in Iraq and for months threatened to overwhelm the Lebanon. On the basis of the Eisenhower Doctrine, American armed forces landed in the Lebanon at the request of the beleagured President of that country, while Britain responded to a similar appeal from King Hussein of Jordan. Civil war between Republicans and Royalists broke out in the Yemen, and Egypt a month later was heavily involved in armed intervention on the side of the Republicans. In an abortive attempt to assassinate President Nasser, King Saud of Saudi Arabia gave Colonel Serraj, Head of the Syrian Military Intelligence, a cheque for a million pounds sterling to place a bomb on the President's plane (Serraj informed Nasser of the plot). Syria lived through a period of increasing tension and instability. It was inevitable that, against the background of political rivalries and passions which engendered these events and were still further heightened by them, the Eisenhower Doctrine seemed a pallid affair, destined to be another damp squib. Above all, it demonstrably ran counter to new trends in the Arab world.

Paradoxically, the dramatic post-Suez decade was, by and large, one of comparative calm as far as the Arab-Israeli conflict was concerned. The United States, which had done so much to render the dangers inherent in that conflict more acute by drawing it into the framework of the Cold War, found itself preoccupied elsewhere, as did the Soviet Union, and with issues of such world significance as Taiwan, Cuba, the Congo, Berlin and Vietnam. And even in the Arab world, where Soviet influence was diligently but discreetly shaping the future and had all but made Arab unity a reality, the Palestine tragedy tended to recede to some extent into the background.

President Kennedy, who as a Senator had described Israel as 'the bright light now shining in the Middle East', was touched to find on his desk, among the hundreds of thousands of congratulatory letters and cables which poured in after his election, a message of greeting from President Nasser, 'from the oldest and poorest country in the world to the youngest and richest'. Kennedy replied courteously and there began a long exchange of correspondence between the two heads of state remarkable for its frankness and mutual sympathy, despite the fact that the writers were more often than not widely at variance in their approach to the world problems they discussed.

But despite the lull in the Arab-Israeli conflict, the coals went on steadily smouldering. Chief among developments of significance in this period were the American decision in the 1960s to become a supplier of major offensive weapons to Israel; and the emergence of the Palestinian people as a recognized independent entity.

In the late 1950s, the United States began to consider abandoning its policy of not supplying arms directly to Israel. If Israel could prove an imbalance in some particular type of weapon, America made it known that she would be ready to re-establish the balance, but not as the main supplier of arms to Israel. Early in the remarkable relationship between Kennedy and Nasser, rumours reached Cairo of American promises to supply Israel with the arms she had for some time been desperately seeking. In 1961, during a visit by Chancellor Adenauer to Washington, Kennedy had in fact persuaded the reluctant West German Chancellor to sell arms to Israel, on the grounds that the United States itself wished to avoid compromising its relationship with the Arab world. Israel received a credit of $60 million from Federal Germany for this purpose; but the American role in the affair did not become known to the Arabs for another four years. Meanwhile the Kennedy administration continued to resist Zionist-Israeli pressures (although frequently paying lip-service, with Vice-President Johnson as spokesman, to Israel and her aspirations). But, on 26 September 1962, Washington announced that the United States had agreed to sell Israel short-range defensive ground-to-air Hawk missiles. This was the first time that America had departed from her policy of letting her European allies serve as arms suppliers to the Zionist state.

In 1957, at a time when Eisenhower and Dulles were contemplating the prospect of putting serious pressure on Israel to withdraw from Gaza and Sharm al-Sheikh, Lyndon Baines Johnson, as majority Senate leader, had told the President that the Senate would never approve punitive sanctions against Israel, while to Dulles he had condemned the threat of sanctions as 'unwise, unfair and one-sided'. As Vice-President, he had visited Israel and had often been delegated by President Kennedy to maintain the administration's contacts with American Zionist organizations. One of his first official acts had been to address the B'nai Zion in New York, on which occasion he had called for a general reduction of Middle East armaments. Mrs Johnson meanwhile roused Arab diplomatic protests when she accepted the honorary chairmanship of an Israel independence ball in Washington in aid of a bond drive. And early in his presidency, Johnson addressed a Weizmann Institute dinner in New York and announced that the United States had offered to co-operate with Israel in using nuclear power to help solve the water shortage problem in the Middle East. The President was enthusiastically cheered by the dinner guests for his repeated sympathetic references to Israel. There seemed, in short, little chance of a truly even-handed Middle East policy, despite frequent assertions by the new administration that, continuing traditional policy, its aim was, first, to avoid in so far as possible selling new arms to the parties in the Arab-Israeli conflict, and secondly, to abstain from any sale of arms which would give one party advantage over the other. In June 1964 President Johnson received the Israeli Prime Minister, Levi Eshkol, and reportedly assured him that the United States stood four-square behind Israel and would not stand idle if she were attacked. No absolute guarantee was given, but machinery was created for joint consultation on political and military levels. In the spring of 1965, the American ambassador in Cairo, Lucius Battle, handed President Nasser a communication announcing that the United States government was now prepared to sell further limited quantities of arms to Israel, provided Israel abstained from launching a preventive action; the Arabs should, however, understand that if they made a major issue of the sale, this might give rise to public reaction which would compromise the American government's impartial approach to the Arab-Israeli problem and discourage it from maintaining its limitation of arms sales to Israel. Additionally, President Johnson wanted President Nasser to know that the United States had decided to sell certain types of weapon to Jordan, to avoid the probable alternative of an offer of arms to that country by the Soviet Union.

This communication, with its hint of double blackmail, inevitably widened the growing gap between the United States and much of the Arab world.

More diplomatically, the State Department tried to clarify the question of arms sales to the Middle East in a statement issued on 5 February 1966. The established United States policy, it said, had been

> to refrain from becoming a major supplier of arms in this area, while retaining the option of helping the countries of the area meet their defence requirements through occasional selective sales.
>
> These exceptions to our general policy have been based on careful case by case examinations and a determination that such a sale would not be a destabilizing factor.
>
> The United States has made over the years repeated quiet efforts to encourage limitations on arms buildups in the area. Until those bear fruit, however, the United States cannot be indifferent to the potentially destabilizing effect of massive Soviet sales of arms to the area.
>
> Over the years, to meet modernization requirements, we have sold the Government of Israel various items of military equipment to help it meet its own defence and internal security requirements. These have included Patton tanks....

In June 1966, Eshkol publicly announced* as Israel's Prime Minister that he had received an undertaking from the United States to safeguard the balance of power in the Middle East – a step that he described as 'a revolution in American thinking'.

* At the First Congress of Rafi party, the political party founded by Ben Gurion when he left the Mapai party at the end of 1964.

A second development of significance in the Arab-Israeli conflict during the post-Suez decade was the creation of a 'Palestinian entity'. In January 1964, President Nasser organized the first Arab 'summit' in an attempt to draw the heat out of the Palestine question; for he had for some time been counselling restraint, while sweetening the pill by assuring his audiences that, in the long run, co-existence with Israel was impossible, and reminding them that the Moslems had had to wait seventy years for their first victory over the Crusaders. Nasser now wanted to force the Arab governments to face up to the cold reality of their responsibilities, instead of contenting themselves with bragadoccio and empty threats. He also wished to offer the Palestinians, who by this stage felt they had little to lose, an opportunity of giving expression to their desire for total opposition to Israel in a form that did not necessarily embarrass the Arab States. A united Arab military command was set up; and it was decided that a Palestinian entity, specifically excluded from taking shape as a government, should be organized. Nasser's choice for this job – bitterly opposed by the previous nominal leader of the Palestinians, Haj Amin el Husseini, former Grand Mufti of Jerusalem – was a Palestinian lawyer, Ahmed Shukairy, who had successively represented Syria and Saudi Arabia at United Nations meetings, where he had for years exhausted delegates by his tendency to get carried away on the tides of his own eloquence. In May 1964, a Palestine National Congress in Jerusalem founded the Palestine Liberation Organization (P.L.O.), with Shukairy as president; soon after, the P.L.O. set up a Palestine Liberation Army from recruits among the refugees in the UNRWA camps and scattered throughout the Arab world.

Despite the Arab states' intention to form a virtually harmless organization (since it depended on the support of the governments where the refugees mainly lived, and since it was headed by a man who, for all his sincerity, had little real influence), the P.L.O., born of a passionate demand for real and immediate action against Israel, soon began to take on an identity and importance of its own. Moreover, to the dismay of the Arab governments (with the exception of Syria), rival Palestinian movements, a few of which had been in existence for some time, became active in terrorist attacks on Israel. Chief among them was al Fath, with its commando organization al Asifa, 'the Storm'. Al Fath (short for Harakat Tahreer Falasteen – Front for the Liberation of Palestine) was formed at Stuttgart University in West Germany by three Palestinian students who had all been active in leftist and nationalist movements since their schooldays in Cairo and Beirut and had been close observers of the Algerian war of liberation. One of them, Yasser Arafat, had become convinced that, unless the Palestinians fought their own battles, there was no chance of their homeland ever being liberated. He fully understood that, by themselves, the Palestinians could not defeat the Israelis, but he felt sure that the first step was to bring world attention to bear on Palestinian claims and that the best way of achieving this was through guerrilla warfare against Israel. Branches of al Fath were soon founded clandestinely in universities in Europe and the Middle East and recruits were sent abroad for training. The group began operations along Israel's border in the early 1960s.

On a less spectacular plane, but possibly of deep import for the future of the Palestinians, was the recognition by UNRWA in the mid-1950s that attempts to solve the refugee problem by trying to promote development schemes in the Arab host countries were doomed to failure. A few years later, the fact had to be faced that even the piecemeal approach of endeavouring to get refugee families on their feet through individual grants had but little impact on the persisting relief problem. Attention shifted to the pressing need for at least the younger generation of refugees to have some chance of a brighter future and earning their living in dignity and independence. Working jointly with Unesco, which provided expert advice, UNRWA accordingly greatly expanded its vocational training programme and steadily enlarged its elementary and junior preparatory school system. The expansion was dramatic: the agency's expenditure on education rose from $300,000 in 1950 to $22.5 million in 1971. By June 1972, over 314,000 refugee children were attending school, for the most part in UNRWA–Unesco schools; nearly 2,700 young men and women were enrolled in UNRWA's vocational training schools and more than 1,000 in its teacher-training centres; nearly 5,000 teachers already working in UNRWA schools had already benefited from UNRWA–Unesco 'in-service' training courses; and 687 students were attending universities in the Middle East, studying mainly such subjects as medicine and engineering. From the standpoint of the young refugees' future, vocational and teacher training facilities form a key programme; the technical subjects are carefully geared to the needs of the expanding economies of the Middle East countries and school teachers are in high demand, so that the young people are afforded solid opportunities for future work.

The United States – by far the most generous supporter of UNRWA (over the years it has contributed on average 70 per cent of the agency's budget, and by December 1972 it had, since May 1950, given UNRWA funds totalling $525,224,592) has always encouraged UNRWA's emphasis on education and training. Addressing the eighteenth session of the General Assembly's Special Political Committee, the American delegate, Mr Cook, declared:

> In years to come, countless young Palestinians, instead of growing up without educational skills to face a hopeless and barren future will take their places in the world as useful and productive citizens; and their contribution to a developing and progressive Middle East will be due in no small measure to the education provided by UNRWA.

This was said in 1963 when UNRWA was looking after an indigent, bewildered and basically diffident multitude of refugees, still nostalgically regretting their past. Now, through the establishment of the Palestine Liberation Movement, it has to deal with a self-confident, forward-looking community. Ironically, an agency designed by its most important sponsor, the United States, to sweep the refugee problem under the carpet by bringing about the absorption of the Palestinians in the Arab countries has, through its education programmes, contributed to the refugees' growing political maturity and national solidarity.

During the second half of 1966, there was a marked increase in the number and importance of Palestine guerrilla raids into Israel from Syria, with the wholehearted support of the new radical government which had come to power in Damascus early that year and which enjoyed strong Soviet backing. The Israeli Chief of Staff, General Rabin, publicly declared that the Syrians were 'the spiritual fathers of the al Fath group'. His warning that Israel's retaliatory measures would be directed against the Syrian régime was echoed by the Prime Minister, Eshkol. The Syrian Prime Minister retorted that his country was not 'the leash that restrains the revolution of the displaced and persecuted Palestinian people' and began talks with President Nasser which resulted, on 4 November, in the signature of a joint Syrian-Egyptian defence agreement.

But when Israel struck it was not at Syria, sheltered to some extent by the Soviet shadow, but at Jordan. On 13 November, Israeli forces attacked and all but demolished the village of Samua, south of Hebron. Jordanian troops intervened, and during the three-hour battle, in which eighty Israeli tanks and twelve aircraft took part, eighteen Jordanians were killed and 134 wounded. In New York the United States voted for a Security Council resolution sternly censuring Israel, and Arthur Goldberg, American representative, told the Council that the Government of Israel had carried out

> a raid into Jordan the nature of which and whose consequences far surpass the cumulative total of the various acts of terrorism conducted against the frontiers. . . . On behalf of my government I wish to make it clear that this large-scale military action cannot be justified, explained away or excused by the incidents which preceded it, in which the Government of Jordan has not been implicated.

The reaction of the Palestinians in Jordan was violent and the army had great difficulty in restoring order. To deflect the blame, King Hussein accused President Nasser of remaining passive and sheltering behind the UNEF forces.

The spring of 1967 brought a recrudescence of the usual exchanges of fire in the demilitarised zone along the Israel–Syria border. Israel had, despite United Nations protests, long disregarded the clause in the 1949 Armistice Agreement which allowed the Arab civilian inhabitants of the zone to continue to live there and cultivate their lands. The Israelis regularly moved in, in spring and autumn, to plough and cultivate these lands and the Syrians as regularly fired on them. In the feverish atmosphere of 1967, these almost traditional exchanges of fire led for the first time to the intervention of aircraft; Israeli planes flew over the suburbs of Damascus and reportedly shot down six Syrian MIGs. The Arabs had suffered their second severe blow in six months and both Syria and Jordan hastened to point out that Egypt had, once again, not stirred a finger.

The situation grew increasingly ominous when Eshkol, having for months been accused of pusillanimity by the activist group in Israel (led by Ben Gurion and Dayan), made a series of belligerent statements culminating in a declaration on 13 May that it was clear that Syria was the focal point of the terrorists, 'but we have laid down the principle that we shall choose the time, the place and the means to counter the aggressor'. The day before the *New York Times* correspondent in Tel-Aviv had reported that some Israeli leaders had decided that the use of force against Syria might be the only way to curtail increasing terrorism. The first official comment by the United States came on 16 May, when Arthur Goldberg told the Security Council that his government was urging restraint on all parties, hoping that its efforts would be met with a constructive response. Meanwhile in Moscow, as the Premier, Mr Kosygin, was later to recall, the Soviet government began receiving information to the effect that the Israeli government had timed for the end of May a swift and crushing strike at Syria, to be followed by an invasion of Egypt. The U.N. Secretary-General, U Thant, gave a warning that recent threatening statements by senior Israeli officials 'could only heighten emotions and increase tensions on the other side of the lines'; and the State Department expressed concern to the Israeli authorities about the inflammatory nature of their reported observations.

In such an atmosphere it was not surprising that rumours were rife. In Syria and Egypt there were many who, recalling Guatemala, Ghana, Indonesia and Greece, believed that the United States, through the C.I.A., now intended to overthrow left-wing régimes in the Eastern Mediterranean, starting with Syria, and probably in collusion with Israel. If such suspicions seem fantastic, it must be remembered that the Arabs were hopelessly confused by what seemed to them the multiplicity of voices through which the United States spoke: the White House said one thing, the State Department often seemed to say another, the Pentagon disagreed, Congress had its own point of view and the C.I.A. meanwhile appeared to pursue an entirely independent policy. Eshkol, by boasting of American support and pointing to the presence of the Sixth Fleet in the Mediterranean, added fuel to the fire. At this juncture word was put about, and widely believed, that Israel was concentrating troops on the Syrian frontier. The Israelis denied this and the United Nations military observers confirmed the absence of any such troop concentrations or movements. Later the claim was made that Soviet intelligence agents had got hold of Israeli military contingency plans and conveyed them to Nasser as plans for a real attack. Other even more devious suppositions have been put forward. What seems clear is that the Soviet Union definitely intended to bring in Nasser to save Syria – not for the purposes of war, but as a show of strength, an essay at brinkmanship, a concrete demonstration of Arab solidarity which Moscow hoped might deter Israel from aggression. Quite apart from loudly proclaimed threats from Tel-Aviv, the Syrian régime was tottering because of a domestic crisis on a religious issue. The U.S.S.R. had managed to develop closer ties with Syria than with any other non-Communist country; the Syrian government depended more and more on Russian aid and held out the best chances for Soviet influence to make itself felt in the region. It was virtually impossible for Nasser, smarting under taunts from Damascus and Amman, to make no response. From then on the die was cast and events became uncontrollable, even by the Super-powers.

On 15 May, when Israel was celebrating the anniversary of its foundation by a military parade in Jerusalem – in defiance of the United Nations and in flagrant contravention of the armistice agreement – Cairo's central districts were being crossed by troops, armoured cars and trucks bound for the Sinai Peninsula and Israel's border. The Chief of the Egyptian General Staff had already arrived in Damascus to symbolize to the Syrians Egypt's support. Next day, the Egyptian President declared a state of emergency.

It is not known whether it was with or without Soviet approval that Nasser took his next fateful steps. Not only in Jordan and Syria, but in Egypt itself, he was being mocked for hiding behind the UNEF. On 16 May, the Egyptian Chief of Staff asked the Indian Commander of UNEF to withdraw his forces from the Sinai border, since Egyptian troops were already concentrated on the border ready for action in the event of Israeli aggression against any Arab country. With a rapidity which Washington felt was an act of folly, U Thant announced that United Nations forces could not remain in Sinai without Egyptian approval, while simultaneously he declared that he would have no choice – UNEF being in his view indivisible – but to withdraw the force also from the Gaza Strip (which Egypt had not at that time requested). President Johnson was deeply disturbed by the Secretary-General's 'ill-conceived' manoeuvre, and angry comment in Congress blasted it as 'a shocking development' and a 'capitulation'.

On 22 May, Nasser took his second fateful step and announced the blockade of the Straits of Tiran. He surely knew that this second step was a desperate one, but he seemed to be impelled, as though by a malevolent destiny, to act in a way he himself had hitherto prudently rejected. Its immediate result was that his prestige soared: the whole Arab world was aflame with enthusiasm; their hero had recovered full sovereignty over all of Egypt's territory and wiped out the last trace of Israel's victory in the Suez War. On behalf of the

Palestinians, Ahmed Shukairy surpassed himself in reckless demagoguery. His wild calls for the extermination of the population of Israel, men, women and children, received full publicity in Western countries and did much to generate enthusiasm there for Israel's cause.

Basically the policy of the United States at this period of crisis was to reach an understanding with Russia that the two super-powers should not interfere. Some months earlier, President Johnson had asked that a special study of Soviet penetration in the Middle East, and its repercussions on the policy and strategy of America and her allies, should be made under the direction of Ambassador Julius Holmes. The study had convinced him that 'the danger implicit in every border incident in the Middle East was not merely war between Israelis and Arabs but an ultimate confrontation between the Soviet Union and the United States and its Nato allies'. A major war had to be avoided at all costs. President Johnson believed that the United States 'had been fair over the years in Middle East matters'. But whether from personal conviction or from what he felt were domestic political imperatives, he remained a firm friend and supporter of Israel. He did not understand that the war which menaced was not due, as he put it in a message to Kosygin, to 'the increasing harassment of Israel by elements based in Syria', but had its roots in events going back fifty years or more – in fact to the concept of a Zionist state in Palestine. And it is not certain how the United States would have acted had the President not been able to tell the Israeli Foreign Minister, Abba Eban, that 'all our intelligence people are unanimous that if the U.A.R. attacks, you will whip hell out of them'.

The President's message to the Soviet Premier, sent on 22 May, suggested a joint effort to calm the situation. 'Your and our ties to nations of the area could bring us into difficulties which I am confident neither of us seeks,' the message ran. 'It would appear a time for each of us to use our influence to the full in the cause of moderation, including our influence over action by the United Nations.' The same day Johnson wrote to Nasser urging him to avoid war as his first duty and announcing that he planned, unless hostilities broke out in the next few days, to send Vice-President Humphrey to talk to the Egyptian President and other Middle East leaders 'in a new attempt to find a solution to the old problem there'. Johnson had already cabled Eshkol urging restraint, and a few days later he told Eban that the central point was that Israel should not be responsible for any outbreak of war. But he added 'very slowly and very positively: "Israel will not be alone unless it decides to go it alone" '.

By then the blockade of the Straits of Tiran had been announced and Johnson had sought former President Eisenhower's confirmation that the Israelis' right of access to the Gulf of Aqaba had been part of the American 'commitment' to Israel in 1957, in return for Israel's withdrawal. On 23 May, the President branded the blockade as 'illegal and potentially disastrous to the cause of peace'. Meanwhile the Secretary of State, Dean Rusk, reported that there was general agreement in Congress that the Arabs should not be allowed to drive the Israelis into the sea. Every government in the world maintaining military attachés in Israel knew that there was no chance of this, but the general public in most countries had reached a high pitch of emotional commitment to what they felt was Israel's cause. In the United States, polls revealed 55 per cent firmly on the side of Israel, and only 4 per cent sympathizing with the Arabs.* But the public as a whole, feeling that the evil of the Vietnam War sufficed unto the day, was not prepared to go as far as backing armed intervention, though American Zionists campaigned for it to happen. The *New York Times* carried an advertisement calling for action 'with nerve and firmness of intent'.

In Moscow the government too was working for moderation. Mr Kosygin told Shans Badran, the Egyptian Minister for War: 'We are ready to support you. But you have already

* Pro-Zionist feeling ran even higher in France (58 per cent for Israel, 2 per cent for the Arabs), despite De Gaulle's chilly policy towards Israel; thousands demonstrated nightly in Paris, shouting 'Nasser to the gallows'. In the Netherlands, as many as 67 per cent came out in favour of Israel and none backed the Arabs.

succeeded in imposing your point of view. You have won a political victory.' By an unlucky quirk of fate, Badran misunderstood what the Soviet Premier was saying and subsequently gave Nasser the impression that the Russians were ready to give him all-out support, including armed support.* When on 27 May Nasser was woken at three-thirty in the morning by a visit from the Russian Ambassador, who had come at the order of the Supreme Soviet to beg the Egyptian President not to fire the first shot, the point of no return had already been reached. Not that Nasser had any intention of aggression, but events were already slipping beyond the point at which they could be controlled.

In Israel, the Egyptian troop concentrations in Sinai had already provoked general mobilization. Confusion reigned: the army wished for quick action against the enemy; the government, although it did not anticipate military defeat, feared heavy civilian air-raid casualties. It decided, therefore, to launch a last-minute diplomatic campaign against invasion threats and more particularly against the blockade of the straits. But by the first days of June it had become clear that concerted action on freedom of navigation, urged with special fervour by the Labour government in Britain, aroused no general enthusiasm among Western Powers. The United States and the United Kingdom were manifestly unable to act alone. In the widespread anxiety in Israel, the Eshkol administration was castigated for inefficiency and inaction. The inclusion in the Cabinet of Colonel Dayan, looked on as the symbol of national self-confidence, virtually became a necessity; but it none the less required a week of political bargaining. Meanwhile Hussein adhered to the common cause and Iraqi troops entered Jordan. To Tel-Aviv it seemed that Israel no longer had room to manoeuvre.

On 5 June at seven in the morning the Israeli air force struck. In less than two hours they had to all intents and

* Heikal, in his book *The Cairo Documents* (p. 190), says, however, that Nasser was subsequently shown the minutes of Badran's conversation with Kosygin, but by then had already made a speech referring to Soviet support.

purposes wiped out the Arab air forces. The war was already virtually won and six days later Israel had redrawn the map of the Middle East. It had conquered and occupied territory belonging to Egypt, Syria and Jordan totalling four times the area allocated to it by the 1949 Armistice Agreements.

In the early morning of 5 June, the 'hot line' – the special teletype circuit linking Moscow and Washington – was in political operation for the first time in history. Premier Kosygin was on the line to President Johnson, expressing concern about the fighting and his intention to work for a cease-fire. The President replied that the United States would use all its influence to bring the fighting to an end, and that he welcomed the Soviet intention to do the same.

At the United Nations that morning, Ambassador Goldberg made the United States's position clear: to achieve the lifting of the blockade of the Gulf of Aqaba, and to compel the withdrawal of Egyptian, as well as Israeli forces, from the Sinai Peninsula. The Egyptians naturally objected to their troops stationed in their own country being treated as an enemy army of occupation, so initially no progress was made in New York. Meanwhile the Israeli Army moved steadily into Jordan and Sinai. The Security Council then adopted a succession of resolutions calling for a cease-fire, with no reference to withdrawal. During the next four days, in President Johnson's words, the peace of the world walked a tightrope. First the Soviet government introduced in the council a new resolution condemning Israel's aggression and her violations of the cease-fire resolutions. By 9 June, Egypt and Jordan had accepted the cease-fire and the United States was using all its diplomatic resources to compel Israel to work out an effective agreement with Syria. One was, indeed, arranged in the early hours of the morning of 10 June. But, shortly afterwards, the hot line was again active, this time with a message from Kosygin accusing Israel of ignoring the Security Council's resolutions and warning that unless she unconditionally halted operations within the next few hours, the Soviet Union would take 'necessary actions, including military'. President Johnson ordered the Sixth Fleet, forbidden up till then to approach nearer than a hundred miles to the Syrian coast, to change course at once and cut their restriction to fifty miles. The message was sufficiently clear without words: the United States was prepared to resist by force Soviet intervention in the Middle East.

Mercifully, soon afterwards Moscow became convinced that the Israeli-Syrian cease-fire would be honoured by Israel, and tension subsided as rapidly as it had built up. In his last hot-line message that morning, Johnson felt able to express hope that the future efforts of both countries would be devoted to achieving lasting peace throughout the world. Nine days later, the President translated this aspiration into Middle East terms. Addressing the National Foreign Policy Conference for Educators on 19 June, he defined five principles which he believed could shape a peaceful Middle East. Convinced that the Israelis, victors though they were, would have to play their part in providing a basis of dignity for their neighbours, he defined these principles as:

the recognized right of national life;
justice for the refugees;
innocent maritime passage;
limits on the wasteful and destructive arms race; and
political independence and territorial integrity for all.

2

The actual result of the war was, in fact, that any hope of a peaceful settlement receded still further into the dim future. Tragically, Israel turned down a unique opportunity to show generosity from its position of strength, confounding even those optimists who had reasoned that it was against the interests and indeed the very purpose of the Zionist state to saddle itself with a huge additional Arab population, now more bitterly hostile than ever. But with every passing month, Israel's determination to hang on to the 'new territories' seemed to become more unyielding.

The Arab states were profoundly shaken. Though the Egyptian people refused to accept Nasser's resignation, he was never to recover his former prestige or power. Jordan had fought bravely, but had emerged on the verge of economic collapse through massive loss of territory, assets and income. Syria and Lebanon were discredited, the one for having failed to make a determined stand on the Israel frontier, the other for ignominiously keeping out of the battle altogether.

Above all, the emotional shock to the Palestinians was overwhelming. More than 300,000 of them, including some 120,000 refugees registered with UNRWA, were reported in the weeks following the war to have lost their homes or to have fled from them (many for the second time in their lives), unable to face the bitter humiliation of life in their own country under an alien government. Pleading for the understanding and financial help of the international community, the commissioner-general of UNRWA, Laurence Michelmore, pointed out that

the disruption of the lives and careers of countless persons, the anxiety caused by the sudden loss of earnings and remittances from abroad, the personal tragedies resulting from the separation of husbands and wives, parents and children, are only some of the problems which confront the former Arab inhabitants of Palestine.

For some weeks that summer, world attention centred on the plight of the refugees. Generous and desperately needed help poured in, above all to UNRWA and to East Jordan, to which the bulk of the refugees had flown and where they were living in conditions of appalling hardship. To lessen the disruption caused by this second Palestinian exodus, the United Nations General Assembly, the Security Council, the Secretary-General and Commissioner-General of UNRWA all urged that those who fled in panic should be allowed to return to their homes. In July, the Government of Israel indicated willingness to allow this, in so far as refugees from West Jordan were concerned, and with the exception of persons whom it regarded as security risks. In the event, out of the 150,000 individuals who, through questionnaires, had made known their wish to return, only some 14,000 were actually allowed to do so by Israel. Among them were a mere 3,000 UNRWA-registered refugees.* Almost no residents of Jerusalem, of UNRWA camps on the West Bank or of the emergency camps set up in East Jordan after the conflict, were permitted to go back. Those who had crossed westwards over the River Jordan joined their hapless brother refugees – some 580,000 of them – to live under military government, as the second-class Arab citizens of Israel had been living for nineteen years.

Israel had continued the laws of mandatory Palestine, including the Defence Emergency Regulations of 1945, drafted when Britain, still at war with Nazi Germany, faced the eruption of widespread Jewish terrorism in Palestine. At that time almost every section of the Jewish community of Palestine and all its leading lawyers had vehemently protested against the inhumanity of the regulations and their violation of elementary human rights; in the words of a future Judge of the Israel Supreme Court, they contradicted 'the most fundamental principles of law, justice and jurisprudence'. Mr Yaacov Shapiro, at the moment of writing Israel's Minister of Justice, described them in 1946 as 'unparalleled in any civilized country; there were no such laws even in Nazi Germany'. He is now applying them to the Arab inhabitants of the occupied territories as well as to the Arab citizens of Israel.

Apart from an isolated case in 1951 when some Orthodox Jews suspected of burning cars travelling on the Sabbath were detained under the regulations, they have never been applied to Jews; as President Pompidou reportedly remarked during his visit to the United States in February 1970, Israel is a racist and religious state. The Defence Regulations are the legal basis for the military government under which the Arabs in Israel have lived since the establishment of the state and

* In many cases some family members had been given permits to return and others had not; and rather than face indefinite separation, the families had preferred to remain in Jordan.

which now rules life in the occupied areas. Under it a military commander has absolute power to exile any person, imprison him, seize his property or place him under house arrest; there is no appeal against the commander's decisions. Until 1965, those Arabs living in certain parts of the country – areas destined for new Jewish settlement – had to seek permission to leave or re-enter their own villages. Apart from such harassment, and from political repression and unequal work and education opportunities, Israel had by the end of 1966 seized about 385 square miles of land from the Arabs who remained there, quite apart from taking possession of the 6,284 square miles of land – an area somewhat larger than Yorkshire – which, according to the United Nations, belonged to the refugees. They had taken the land from the resident Arabs by forcible expropriation and by the enaction of a series of laws and orders, the main purpose of which was to justify retrospectively acts of seizure that had already been carried out, and to give the authorities power to expropriate such land as still remained in Israeli Arab hands. During the first ten years of Israel's existence, the inhabitants of over thirty Arab villages were forcibly expelled, their houses demolished and their lands expropriated. Compensation was paid, but by a trick the Israel government gained possession of the land for practically nothing, for the relevant law, dated 1953, stipulated that values obtaining on 1 January 1950 should form the basis of compensation. In January 1950 practically no sales of land had as yet taken place and prices were very low; further, the Israeli pound was then equivalent to the pound sterling, whereas by the time the law was passed it was worth only 20 per cent of the pound.

There was therefore little hope that anything but harsh treatment would be meted out to the Arabs who after the June War found themselves living under Israeli occupation, principally in the Gaza Strip and West Jordan. The Special United Nations Committee set up to investigate their treatment in so far as human rights were concerned found evidence reflecting a policy on the part of the Government of Israel designed to effect radical changes in the physical character and demographic composition of several areas of the territory under occupation by the progressive and systematic elimination of every vestige of Palestinian presence in those areas.

This, the committee declared, would have the effect, contrary to international law, of transforming the areas concerned into parts of the Jewish state. 'The right of the inhabitants of the occupied territories to remain in their homeland is unqualified and inalienable.' The committee condemned the recurring imposition of dawn-to-dusk curfews (involving intolerable hardships in refugee huts with only communal water and sanitation facilities); the deportation of several hundred Arabs from their homes; the mass displacement of some 15,000 other Arab residents; the arbitrary destruction of the houses of persons suspected of helping members of the resistance; the destruction of Arab villages; the establishment of forty-five Israeli settlements in the occupied territories since the 1967 war. It found that these practises were a violation of fundamental human rights. On the basis of testimony received, the committee concluded that the Government of Israel was carrying out these policies with the ultimate object of annexing and settling the occupied territories.

However, alongside all this harassment and distress, the Palestinians under Israel's control and outside it experienced, as a result of the war, a great upsurge of hope and self-confidence. The most significant outcome of the war seemed at the time – and may in the future appear so again – to be the resurgence and new independence of the Palestine national movement. Indeed the Arab peoples as a whole, humiliated by the defeat of their regular armies, gave the resistance fighters their support and sympathy. Shukairy disappeared from the scene at the end of the hostilities and his place as leader of the resistance movement was taken by Yasser Arafat. The Palestinian groups grew steadily in independence and maturity and became a new political power in the Middle East. For the first time, an Arab group formulated a programme in the event of an Arab victory. The Palestinians wanted the destruction of the Zionist state and in its place a democratic Palestine with equal rights for all inhabitants, Jewish and Arab. Al Fath, the largest of the resistance groups, did not become fully active or widely known until after the June War. At this point a separate, smaller and more extremist group, the Popular Front for the Liberation of Palestine, came into being. Its leadership was predominantly Christian, Beirut-educated and intellectual. It was headed by George Habbache, a Palestinian doctor in his early forties who was in charge of an Amman clinic run by a group of nuns and caring mainly for refugees from the nearby camps. The Popular Front's activities were based on the idea that the enemy (by whom they meant Israel and 'American imperialism') was vulnerable to attack in any part of the world and that if such attacks resulted in headlines in the press, this would be all to the good; the world had for too long been completely oblivious of the Palestinians. The group had the same general aim as the Palestine Liberation Movement as a whole, but in addition had the objective of overthrowing reactionary régimes throughout the Arab world.

After months of patient negotiation, the Security Council in November 1967 came up with a resolution introduced by Britain and which, by a miracle, was nominally accepted by nearly all the parties directly or closely concerned; the U.A.R., Jordan, the Lebanon, Israel, the United States and the Soviet Union. The only exceptions were Syria and the Palestinians. Except that it made no reference to arms limitation, the resolution incorporated the substance of four of President Johnson's five principles, though almost its every word had been haggled over and redrafted countless times. In its resolution the Security Council emphasized the inadmissibility of the acquisition of territory by war, the need to work for a lasting peace in which every state in the area could live in security and the commitment of all member states of the United Nations to act in accordance with Article 2 of the Charter (the obligation to settle disputes by peaceful means and to refrain from the threat or use of force); and went on to affirm that a 'just and lasting peace' in the Middle East should include the application of the following principles:

the withdrawal of Israeli armed forces from territories occupied in the recent conflict; and

the termination of all claims or states of belligerence and respect for and acknowledgement of the sovereignty, territorial integrity and political independence of every state in the area and their right to live in peace within secure and recognized boundaries free from threats or acts of force.

The council also affirmed the necessity for guaranteeing freedom of navigation through international waterways in the area; for achieving a just settlement of the refugee problem; and for guaranteeing the territorial inviolability and political independence of every state in the area, through measures including the establishment of demilitarized zones. Finally, it asked the Secretary-General to appoint a special representative to assist efforts of the parties to achieve a settlement in accordance with the above provisions and principles. The hapless holder of this post, Gunnar Jarring, Swedish Ambassador to the Soviet Union, is still after more than five years intermittently shuttling to and fro between New York and the Middle East capitals, or waiting in the wings.

The sponsors of the resolution believed that it held out real prospects for a settlement, since it offered to each party a chance of fulfilling their essential objectives: to Israel, security; to the Arabs, withdrawal of Israel from occupied territories and a 'just settlement' of the refugee problem. Unhappily, the resolution had two fatal weaknesses: though it acknowledged a need for a just solution of the refugee problem (a concept which, to many, is excluded in advance by the establishment of an alien state in the refugees' country) it failed to come to grips with the fundamental problem, the just treatment of the claims and aspirations of the Palestinian people as a whole. In President Nasser's words, it was 'inadequate to fulfil the Palestinian destiny'; and the Central Committee of al Fath warned that any resolution which ignored the basic fact of the national rights of the Palestinians would be doomed to failure. Secondly, it meant all things to all men. Not only could the phrase 'a just settlement of the refugee problem' be interpreted in a hundred different ways, but the crucial question of Israel's withdrawal from the lands she had occupied as a result of the June War meant totally different things to different parties. To Israel, and also to the United States, it meant Israeli withdrawal to frontiers agreed between the parties themselves as part of a comprehensive settlement; to the Arabs, the Soviet Union and most of the U.N. membership, it meant that Israel must withdraw completely and unconditionally to the 1949 armistice lines and, the Arabs added, *before* any discussion regarding a general settlement could begin.

It is obvious that, since the council had declared that it was inadmissible to acquire territory by war, it had intended Israel to withdraw completely and rapidly. But the armistice lines had never been intended to be more than temporary lines enshrined in military agreements which, it was thought at the time, would within a matter of months be superseded by a political settlement laying down fixed frontiers. Both sides could with justice claim that the armistice lines did not provide them with 'secure' boundaries. Inevitably all too soon Israel was claiming that Jerusalem, the Golan Heights and the Gaza Strip were not negotiable; while the U.A.R. was announcing that the maximum area that could be envisaged for Israel was the territory lying within the 1949 demarcation lines. (This was a concession by the Arabs, who had hitherto stood out for the boundaries recommended in the United Nations 1947 partition plan.)

At the end of the June War, Israel failed to take a magnificent opportunity to show, from her position of strength, magnanimity towards her defeated enemies. Possibly she expected early approaches from Egypt and Jordan with a view to sueing for peace. But such an eventuality was made unlikely by the decision of the Soviet Union, almost immediately after the cessation of hostilities, to pour arms into Egypt. Encouraged by this, Nasser reached the conclusion that his first aim should be to gain time and that the U.A.R. should not contemplate any negotiations for a settlement before it had recovered its full strength. By the autumn of 1968, it had been able to concentrate a large and well-equipped force along the Western bank of the Suez Canal. Suddenly one October night the force struck, shelling the Israeli positions massively. Israel responded by a helicopter-carried commando raid deep into Upper Egypt. The 'war' of attrition was on, though it was not officially announced as such until April 1969, when Nasser declared that the U.N.-imposed cease-fire was null and void. By the summer the Israelis had an average casualty rate of seventy a month in the Canal sector alone. Egyptian confidence rose to new heights; but in July 1969 Israel decided to use her U.S.-supplied planes for the first time since the June War, attacking the suburbs of Cairo and Egyptian artillery positions and missile sites. It seemed as if a new all-out war were in sight.

Meanwhile the Palestine conflict had intruded into the American presidential electoral scene. On 4 June 1968 Senator Robert Kennedy, candidate for the Democratic nomination, had been shot in Los Angeles by a twenty-four-year-old Palestinian, Sirhan Bishara Sirhan, who was incensed by Kennedy's pro-Israel stand during the campaign. No connection could be established between the murderer and any other group or individual. The crime took place only two months after the assassination of the civil rights leader, Dr Martin Luther King; and, for the country as a whole, it seemed not so much an unbalanced youth's attempt to focus attention on the plight of the Palestinians as one more consequence of nation-wide lawlessness and criminal contempt for the rights of others. President Johnson had called for the appointment of a commission of distinguished Americans to look into 'this tragic phenomenon'.

One of the first acts of the Nixon administration had been to study exhaustively the entire Middle East situation. Even before his inauguration, the new president had sent William W. Scranton (his original choice for Secretary of State) on a fact-finding mission to the area. Israelis and American Zionists alike were disconcerted when Scranton announced, halfway through his mission, that President Nixon envisaged an 'even-handed' Middle East policy. They recalled the 1956 election slogan, 'A vote for Ike is a vote for Nasser, Nixon and Dulles', and were alarmed at the possibility that Eisenhower's former vice-president might force a new Israeli withdrawal from occupied territories. As President, however, Nixon was looking at the problem from a totally different angle. He had pledged to move from confrontation to negotiation with the Soviets; he saw the Middle East deadlock as the first test of his ability to redeem that pledge. At the request of the newly appointed Secretary of State, William P. Rogers, a position paper had been put forward by the Assistant Secretary of State, Joseph J. Sisco, arguing that the only way to stop the growth of Soviet influence was, first, to bring the conflict to an end, and secondly to put a stop to Arab dependence on Soviet help. The plan, in which the President and his senior aides concurred, was to 'sell' to the parties, through Jarring, an agreed United States–Soviet peace plan, which would necessarily involve Israel's withdrawal from the occupied territories. The President hoped that the Middle East negotiations would pave the way to further, even more vital, discussions with the Russians on general arms limitation. Against the menacing background of escalating hostilities, the United States, therefore, carried on at intervals bi-lateral discussions with Russia and four-power talks with the U.S.S.R., Britain and France (suggested by the French government and the U.N. Secretary-General). In October 1969, the United States submitted a 'final formulation' to the Soviet Union; it was turned down. The hope of imposing an agreed settlement faded and American Zionists redoubled their efforts to secure further military aid for Israel and intensified their campaign for direct Arab-Israeli talks. The first public expression of American policy since the discussions with other governments began showed the extent to which the United States had made concessions, and was anathema to Israel on that account. It came in the form of an address by Rogers, the Secretary of State, to the Galaxy Conference on Adult Education in New York, on 9 December 1969 and was authoritatively described as a 'vitally comprehensive statement of current United States policy on the Middle East'.

On the crucial question of withdrawal, Rogers told his audience: 'We do not support expansionism. We believe troops must be withdrawn as the resolution provides.' But he added a reference to 'insubstantial alterations' in borders required for mutual security. When he reached the main point of the speech – the suggestion that, to break the deadlock, 'one must start somewhere' and that such a start should be an effort to reach an Israel–U.A.R. settlement – he disconcertingly included a reference to Israeli withdrawal from Sinai 'to the international border between Israel and Egypt which has been in existence for over half a century'. Apart from the fact that Israel had been in existence for twenty-one not fifty years, and that the border between Egypt and the area known before 1918 as the Sanjak of Jerusalem had existed for much longer than fifty years, this would have meant accepting Israel's occupation by force of the Gaza Strip, with its 400,000 Palestine Arab inhabitants (administered by Egypt since 1949), in contradiction to the terms of the very resolution which Rogers affirmed was the basis of American policy. The other elements of the plan were that the 'Rhodes formula' be used in negotiations between the parties* and that there should be a mutually binding commitment to peaceful relations. President Nasser accepted the United States proposals, pointing out, however, that they contained nothing that was not already in the Security Council's resolution.

Two weeks later the *New York Times* published the eleven-point American proposals for an Israel–Jordan settlement. Once again, references to Israeli withdrawals were qualified by such phrases as 'substantial withdrawals' and 'approximations' to the armistice line. Other significant points were that Jordan would be committed to preventing Palestine guerrilla raids from her territory; that the fate of Jerusalem, which

---

* The negotiations for the 1949 Armistice Agreements were conducted by the parties on the island of Rhodes, through the good offices of the acting mediator in Palestine, Dr Ralph Bunche.

should in any case be a unified city with roles for both Israel and Jordan in civic, economic and religious life, would be settled by Israel and Jordan; and that each refugee should be given the opportunity of indicating his decision on the question of a return to Israel. On the following day the Secretary of State was asked at a news conference whether America should not refrain from formulating proposals that Israel saw as prejudicing her case. He replied with refreshing firmness that the United States had to conduct its foreign policy 'in a way we think is best for our national interests'.

Mrs Golda Meir, by now Israel's Prime Minister, angrily rejected the American proposals as pro-Arab while her government took the unprecedented step of circulating through its embassy in Washington public denunciations of the Secretary of State's policy statement. The Palestine resistance movement maintained its hostility to any peace initiative that did not acknowledge its direct and paramount involvement in the issue and its determination to prevent a conference-table sellout of its cause. For their part, the Russians objected that the proposals were of a 'one-sided and pro-Israel nature'. The United States, however, pressed on.

Israel's sharp reaction to the war of attrition had given the Soviet Union the opportunity to extend its 'presence' in the U.A.R. At the end of April 1970 an Israeli government communiqué announced that Soviet pilots were carrying out operational raids from Egyptian bases. A few days later, the Israeli Defence Minister, Moshe Dayan, stated that, in his view, the Russians had undertaken the defence of Egypt's vital centres – Cairo, Alexandria and the Aswan area – thus freeing Egyptian forces for heavier attacks on Israeli positions. Washington promptly expressed its concern to Moscow and asked for a clarification of Soviet intentions. But the inevitable chain-reaction continued. Israel stepped up its demands for further Phantom aircraft from the United States. Seventy-nine Senators, both Republicans and Democrats, joined in appealing to Rogers to respond favourably and a majority of the House wrote in the same sense to President Nixon. Meanwhile President Nasser, in a May Day speech, while criticizing in a routine way America's pro-Israel stand in the past, clearly indicated his anxiety for further United States moves to secure a settlement.

What came to be known as the 'Rogers Plan' was first announced by the Secretary of State at a news conference on 25 June 1970, but Mr Rogers gave no details, merely remarking that it was 'an initiative based on the idea of getting the parties to stop shooting'. It came in the form of a letter from the Secretary of State to the Egyptian Foreign Minister, Mahmoud Riad, dated 19 June but not made public till 22 July. The Secretary of State proposed, first, that the U.A.R. and Israel should agree to a restoration of the cease-fire, at least for three months; and secondly that they should subscribe to a statement, in the form of a report from Ambassador Jarring to the U.N. Secretary-General, indicating their agreement to carry out the Security Council's resolution in all its particulars, and be ready to designate representatives to take part in discussions under Jarring's auspices concerning mutual recognition of sovereignty and Israeli withdrawal. A similar letter was sent to the Foreign Minister of Jordan. All three parties accepted the American proposals. It seemed a resounding triumph for Rogers's quiet diplomacy. But, shortly thereafter, Israel withdrew its acceptance on the grounds that the U.A.R. had taken advantage of the new cease-fire to move forward certain surface-to-air missiles. This was denied by Moscow, but Washington later confirmed that the United States had photographic evidence that the missiles had in fact been moved. For the second time the Soviet Union had rebuffed American efforts to achieve a settlement.

During the summer of 1970, the United States retreated both from its earlier stand on the question of withdrawal and the question of aircraft supplies for Israel. It also appeared to reverse its eighteen-year (purely nominal) acceptance in the United Nations in favour of repatriation of the refugees. At a briefing session in the White House, it was explained that it was not to be expected that Israel should agree to take back a million refugees, since this would alter 'the fundamental

Jewish character of the State of Israel'. On 9 June, Rogers told the House Committee on Foreign Affairs that the earlier decision to hold in abeyance Israel's request for more Phantoms had been made in the hope that it would set a pattern of restraint in the Middle East. 'Since it has not done so,' he added, 'we have initiated a new evaluation of the situation.' President Nixon meanwhile made a series of pronouncements in which any pretence to an even-handed attitude was discarded. The United States recognized, he said in a television and radio interview on 1 July, 'that Israel is not desirous of driving any of the other countries into the sea. The other countries do want to drive Israel into the sea.' The President went on to explain his version of the balance of power in the Middle East: 'Once Israel is weaker than its neighbours, there will be a war.' Therefore it was, he suggested, in the interests of the United States to maintain Israel in a position of military superiority and to favour, not Israel's withdrawal from the territories she had conquered in 1967, but her withdrawal to 'borders that are defensible'. The situation in the Middle East, Nixon concluded, was dangerous because it involved a collision of the super-powers. Seventy-one Senators later endorsed this proposition.

Three weeks later, Nixon reverted to the need to maintain his version of the balance of power, 'so that no state would be encouraged to launch an offensive against another state or to be driven to launch a pre-emptive strike, because of fear of an offensive or a build-up'. And replying evasively on 10 December to a question put at a news conference as to whether it remained United States policy that Israel must withdraw from all occupied Arab territories except for what Rogers had described as 'insubstantial alterations', the President said that American policy was founded basically on the Security Council's 1967 resolution:

Now that is a matter for negotiation, and to be more precise than that I do not think would be helpful at this time. I would only say that the cease-fire should continue; that I trust we can get the legislation through for the supplemental ... so that we can keep the balance of power in that part of the world. ...

Mr Rogers had also foreshadowed this development. On 9 October he had explained at a news conference that, though the cease-fire agreement did not prohibit arms supplies, the United States had acted with restraint; it had not provided Israel with more arms than it had previously agreed to supply. But, in view of Soviet military support for Egypt, 'of course we are under no restraint at all' in so far as provision of further arms to Israel was concerned.

During the late summer of 1970, two tragic events had shaken the Middle East: the sudden death of President Nasser, and a savage civil war in Jordan between the régime and the Palestine guerrillas. The resistance movement bitterly opposed Jordan's agreement to enter into the negotiations called for by the Rogers Plan, which, they contended, approached the conflict without reference to its fundamental basis: the eviction of the native population of Palestine from their country. Furthermore, many Palestinians were strongly Marxist or Maoist and determined on the overthrow of the pro-Western Hashemite monarchy. By the end of August, after a series of devastating hijackings of aeroplanes by Palestinian commandos, culminating in the capture by the P.F.L.P. of two American, one Swiss and one British plane and their diversion to Jordan and Egypt, fighting broke out between the guerrillas and the Jordanian army, causing havoc in Amman and in the adjoining huge refugee camps. Syria threatened to send tanks to help the commandos; and the frightening possibility emerged that, should King Hussein seem likely to lose the war, Israel might intervene, smash the Syrian tanks and even attack the Soviet missiles moved up to the Suez Canal by Egypt. Once again the shadow of a Third World War hovered over the Middle East. President Nixon's first step was to order reinforcements of the Sixth Fleet and of American airborne troops in Europe; the Soviet Union had at all costs to be made to realize that if Hussein's fall seemed imminent, the United States would intervene. The plan was, first, to land troops to rescue the hijacked American plane passengers marooned at Zerqa, not far from Amman (the other American plane had been blown up in Cairo after the passengers had been allowed to leave); and then, if Hussein appealed for direct military help, to give it to him. The Syrian tanks in fact crossed the Jordan frontier on 19 and 20 September. The next day it was secretly agreed by President Nixon and the Israeli ambassador, Rabin, that if the tanks reached Amman Israel would attack. It was understood that the United States would protect Israel's rear with the Sixth Fleet. The Soviet Minister in Washington was warned that, if the Syrian tanks were not withdrawn from Jordan, the United States could not predict what action it would take. Entirely unknown outside a very small circle, world peace hung by a very thin thread during those few days. The situation was reversed at the last moment by Hussein's spectacularly successful air and land attack on the tanks; the commandos suffered overwhelming reverses and were banned from operating from Jordan. A direct outcome of the Palestinian defeat was the formation in July 1971 of the Black September guerrilla group.

Many observers felt that the new Egyptian President held out a hope that serious negotiations would shortly begin. But President Sadat soon astonished the world by the dignity and courage with which he tackled his almost impossibly difficult task and by the firmness with which he maintained the Arab position. The American Secretary of State, Rogers, was liked and trusted in Egypt, and many believed that his policies could lead to the kind of settlement with Israel which Egypt could accept. In February 1971, in response to overwhelming pressure from the United States, the U.A.R. responded affirmatively to a new move by Mr Jarring and gave positive commitments on all eight points of a questionnaire, based on the principles and provisions of the Security Council's resolution, which he had submitted to the parties. For its part, Israel replied to the questionnaire by announcing that it would not withdraw to the pre-June 1967 lines and by ignoring all the other points.

President Sadat's 'year of decision' proved, in fact, to be a peak year for Israel. Election year was approaching in the United States. In April, the Israeli Foreign Minister, Abba Eban, jubilantly proclaimed in Washington that the American-Israeli partnership had attained 'the highest degree of mutual confidence and understanding ever known between the two nations'. He outlined three elements of this understanding: no Israeli withdrawal without a negotiated settlement; maintenance of President Nixon's version of the 'balance of power'; no imposition of a peace settlement from outside (i.e. from the Soviet Union or the United Nations). Nixon (for whom in 1968 only one Jewish voter in five had voted) had, it turned out from the 1971 record, done more for Israel than any previous President, at least so far as arms supplies were concerned. American arms sales to Israel that year were reported to have totalled $600 million, compared to the peak of $80 million in President Johnson's 'best year'. And 1971 closed with a further Israeli triumph. On 31 December, shortly after Mrs Meir's rejection of a fresh appeal by the Secretary of State to Israel to withdraw from Arab territories, United States government sources leaked to the press the news that the sales of Phantoms to Israel were to be renewed. The Senate had approved the Foreign Relations Appropriations Bill, which cleared the way for a $50 million grant to assist Israel's budget, and $300 million for military credit sales and low-interest financing of Phantoms and other equipment.

The effect of this news on the Arab world was shattering. Overnight, faith in the trustworthiness of the United States crumbled; the Egyptians saw that they had been cruelly betrayed. The Secretary of State's years of patient efforts had been brought to nothing. America, it seemed, would not find it easy, or perhaps possible, to restore its credibility in the Arab Middle East.

In early 1972, all eyes were turned to President Nixon's Moscow visit. Both sides were apprehensive lest they should be sold down the river by an agreed decision of the two super-powers to impose a settlement. Egypt, in particular, was suspicious of the Soviet Union's new moves to extend its influence in the region, notably in Iraq, and by its evident reluctance to ensure that Egypt would regain the Sinai Peninsula by force of arms. In the event, nothing tangible on the Middle East emerged from the Moscow summit except the remark by the Russian Foreign Minister, Mr Gromyko, in Paris in mid-June to the Foreign Minister of France that the meeting had revealed very deep differences between the United States and the Soviet Union on the region. Various versions of agreed proposals were soon rumoured, among them a scheme for a freeze by both super-powers on all new arms supplies for Israel and Egypt. It was attributed to Dr Kissinger and said to be the chief reason for the Soviet government's calm reaction to the eviction of Russian experts by President Sadat in July 1972. But there was still no answer to the agonizing question of whether, one day, a political grouping would be able to persuade the parties to negotiate a settlement, or whether the Middle East as a whole would continue its tragic and dangerous role as one of the theatres of the Russian-American confrontation.

9. THE ARAB-ISRAELI CONFLICT IN THE 1972 AMERICAN ELECTIONS

When, in the last week of August 1972, the two national political parties had adopted their platforms for the coming election, Republicans and Democrats, as one commentator put it, appeared to differ on every issue, domestic or foreign, with the single exception of total and irremediable commitment to the preservation of Israel's security and the furtherance of her interests.* Even when account was taken of the wide gap between political promises and performance, this extraordinary situation could be counted a joint triumph of Israel's diplomacy and of the power of American Zionists, who had once again proved their ability to pipe a tune to which the nation's representatives were apparently willing to dance. Rabbi Arthur Hertzberg, President of the American Jewish Congress, could claim with some justification that the position of both parties and

* This was a little too sweeping; both parties managed to agree that property taxes should be reduced.

both presidential candidates reflected 'the overwhelming support in the general American public for a safe and secure Israel'. At times during the campaign, Republicans and Democrats seemed in fact to be trying to outdo one another in assurances of friendship for Jews in general and Israel in particular. 'The way American politicians compete to please Israel has become a comedy, perhaps a tragedy,' President Sadat remarked bitterly to the Egyptian Parliament; and even the *New York Times* had earlier observed, during the Florida primary in March, that the real ambition of most Democratic candidates seemed to be to sit in the Knesset in Jerusalem.

The political influence of the American Jewish community grows dramatically with the approach of elections The six million American Jews are numerically insignificant; they form only 3 per cent of the total population of the United States. But they happen to be chiefly concentrated in a few large and highly populated states, notably in New York and California. Each state has the same number of electoral votes as representatives in the House, who in turn are allotted in proportion to the size of the state's population. A presidential election works in each state on the principle of 'all or nothing'; regardless of the size of his popular vote, the winning candidate receives all the state's electoral votes. Mr Truman in 1948, for example, carried California by about 18,000 of the more than four million votes cast in the state, but received all its twenty-five electoral votes. The 'all or nothing' principle puts a big premium on winning those states with the largest populations. New York, California, Pennsylvania, Illinois, Massachusetts and Ohio have between them 178 of the 226 electoral votes needed to win a presidential election and 75 per cent of American Jews are believed to live in those six states (40 per cent in New York City alone). As long ago as 1947, the then Democratic National Committee Chairman, Senator J. Howard McGrath, put the point succinctly; he told the Defence Secretary, James Forrestal, at the time pursuing his lonely campaign to lift the Palestine problem out of American domestic politics, that 'there were two or three pivotal states which could not be carried without the support of people who were deeply interested in the Palestine question'. The situation has not changed since. In 1968, 85 per cent of New York City Jews voted for Senator Hubert Humphrey. Humphrey won New York State by only 371,000 votes, so he might well have lost the state without the Jewish votes.

The Democratic National Committee Chairman was not, of course, thinking in terms of Jewish votes alone, but also of vital financial support for party campaigns. In an article published in England in October 1972, the American diplomat David Nes quotes columnist Joseph Alsop's assertion that, 'with the possible exception of Senator Edward Kennedy, no liberal Democrat gets less than 50 per cent of his financing from the Jewish community. In certain cases, the percentage reaches a very much higher figure.' Nes adds that a reliable estimate places Jewish financial support of Democratic candidates during the 1970 congressional elections at 64 million dollars and observes that, although Presidents Eisenhower and Nixon won without Jewish financial support, political observers find it inconceivable that a Democratic presidential candidate could win without such backing.

Even before the 1972 campaign officially got under way, some American Jews had, however, begun to feel that the Zionist-Israel issue had been magnified to an unwarranted and alarming extent and could wind up by being counter-productive so far as the interests of American Jewry and Israel herself were concerned. In mid-August Rabbi Hertzberg called on Jewish leaders to refrain from attacks on candidates and policies as well as from endorsements of them. Newspapers such as the *Washington Post* and the *Chicago Tribune* were full of letters asking whether the idea that common interests linked the United States and Israel was not just a stunt to win Jewish votes. In the *Los Angeles Times*, Clayton Fritchey asserted that competition for Zionist votes between the two presidential candidates was 'hardly an ideal way to conduct foreign policy. Now is a good time for a moratorium on this.'

The American Jewish community turned out to be more

divided on domestic political issues than it had ever been. For a variety of reasons, the traditional support of the majority of American Jews for the Democratic party was weakening. Among the grounds for this was the growing sense of insecurity which seemed to be developing and which was ascribed to the policies of some Democrats. In certain neighbourhoods, Jews were already alarmed by racial pressures. Many felt threatened in their professional efforts to be recognized on the basis of ability alone. Particularly in New York City, Jewish teachers and other city employees feared that they would lose their jobs through the 'quota' system, the aim of which was to make jobs available to blacks and Puerto Ricans in proportion to the size of these two groups of city residents. Others were worried by the espousal by liberal Democrats of such policies as racial quotas for educational facilities and 'integrated' housing. In Washington, Jewish civil servants who felt that they had won their posts by merit were concerned lest they be forced out of their jobs by the demands of blacks for appointments on a quota basis. McGovern had given the impression that he favoured the proportionate award of federal jobs to blacks (though he later repudiated the quota system).

Higher up the social scale, wealthy and secure Jews viewed with no enthusiasm the Democratic candidate's proposals to close tax loopholes and increase taxes at the higher levels. There was widespread anxiety about the identification of young people, including many young Jews, and of the 'New Left' with the Palestinian cause. Conservative elements in the community, like the majority of conservative-minded Americans, disliked what they considered to be McGovern's radicalism; nor did they feel certain of his long-term support for Israel.

In spite of pleas for an electoral moratorium on Jewish issues, the usual competition for Jewish votes was soon well under way, having been vigorously launched in December 1971 by Senator Hubert Humphrey. During the contest for the Democratic nomination, Humphrey had started a debate on who, among the candidates, had done most for Israel. At a later stage of the campaign, he himself was to be awarded top rating (100 per cent), together with the Republican Minority Leader Hugh Scott and three other Senators, in the first ratings ever made of Senate performance on 'issues of importance to Jews'. Very near the end of the list came Senator Mike Mansfield, Democratic Majority Leader, with a rating of only 8.5, while the chairman of the Senate Foreign Relations Committee, Senator Fullbright, brought up the rear with a zero rating. Senator McGovern himself received a rating of 87.5 and tied for fifteenth place.*

That he achieved even this had all too obviously been the result of heavy pressures brought to bear on him by his campaign managers. When the public opinion polls began to show a definite switch of Jewish voters from the Democratic to the Republican party, the Democrats redoubled their efforts in an attempt to arrest this trend. It was acutely embarrassing for them that their candidate should be suspect in American Zionist eyes because he had been ready to consider the internationalization of Jerusalem, and because of his support of the 1970 Rogers Plan for Israeli withdrawal from occupied territories with only minor frontier adjustments and for the continuation of United Nations peace efforts through Ambassador Jarring. By the end of May 1972, in Los Angeles, McGovern was condemning the Rogers Plan as an attempt to impose a settlement on Israel and calling on the United States to recognize Jerusalem as Israel's capital and to transfer its embassy from Tel Aviv to the Holy City. In June, paying a Democratic candidate's traditional visit to New York's garment centre, heavily populated by Jews, he announced that he wanted

> to lay at rest what I believe to be a cynical, belligerent and unscrupulous effort by my opposition to distort my position with regard to the State of Israel. As president, I would

* The ratings were made by the newly formed National Centre for Jewish Policy Studies on the basis of attitudes taken by Senators during 1969–72 on over twenty issues of 'clear and immediate Jewish interest', including six roll-call votes in the Senate relating to the question of arms to Israel.

see that American aid is available in whatever measure is necessary to see to it that the one free and democratic state in the Middle East survives. I bitterly resent the charge that my opposition to the war in Vietnam somehow means that I do not favour firm American support for Israel. . . . I want you to know that in George McGovern the people and Government of Israel have a dependable friend.

In his acceptance speech at Miami Beach on 14 July he promised that, if he were elected, America would keep its defence forces fully sufficient to meet any danger confronting 'our old allies in Europe and elsewhere including the people of Israel who will always have our help to hold their promised land'. In mid-August, in a telephone interview with the Israel forces radio, he was more specific: he pledged military supplies, especially of fighter aircraft, and promised, if elected, not to impose a settlement. By the end of August he was taking up a more blatantly pro-Israel stand than any other American political leader had publicly adopted in recent years. Heedless of the announced policy of the United States favouring a return to the 1967 pre-war frontiers with only minor adjustments, he called for a complete hands-off attitude on the future Israeli-Egyptian border. As a result, he asserted, of a war not of Israel's choosing, 'certain boundaries were established at that time'. Any change in those boundaries could only come as a result of direct Arab–Israel talks, on which Israel had always insisted. And in a major foreign policy statement, made in part before the City Club of Cleveland on 5 October, he stressed that the Soviet pull-out in Egypt did not end the threat to Israel. 'We must continue to retain sufficient power in the area to ensure that there is no doubt of our commitment to Israel's security.' Much of this was an attempt to refute Republican accusations that the Democratic candidate's call for massive defence cuts made nonsense of his new strongly pro-Israel policy.

Meanwhile two leading members of McGovern's camp had been dispatched in August to Israel. They were Senator

Frank Church of Idaho, a member of the Senate Foreign Relations Committee and a potential Secretary of State under a McGovern administration, and Myer Feldman, who had served Presidents Johnson and Kennedy as adviser on minority relations and had been their special contact with the American Jewish leaders. Pressed to explain the discrepancy between the Democratic candidate's current statements and his earlier support for the Rogers Plan, Church claimed that he was not familiar with McGovern's stand in 1967, but was acquainted with his present attitude, 'and you people have no need for anxiety'. McGovern hoped to reduce overall military expenditure, Church explained, but not at the expense of the Sixth Fleet, which would be maintained in the Mediterranean at its present level. Back home the vice-presidential Democratic candidate Sargent Shriver was accusing the President of playing politics with American-Israeli relations. 'Under four years of Richard Nixon,' he declared, 'we've seen America's commitment to Israel flow with the shifting political tides. We need only look back three years to find Richard Nixon sitting on his hands in the face of Israel's urgent request for Phantom jets.' And by early October, Jewish residential areas were being inundated with a pamphlet entitled *The Nixon record on Israel – Who's he kidding? – The McGovern record of consistent support of Israel – A history of friendship.*

The President did not need to protest so much. Though he, too, had changed direction to Israel's advantage since his vice-presidential stand in 1956 in favour of her withdrawal from Sinai and his determination in 1969, as newly elected president, to follow an 'even-handed' policy in the Middle East, even to compromising on almost every issue except Israel's actual existence, his current strongly pro-Israel attitude could not be feared to be merely a matter of election campaign tactics. During the previous two years his administration's lavish arms supplies and sustained political support for Israel, in and out of the United Nations, had earned the gratitude of the Zionists. In Washington Israel's Ambassador, General Rabin, had declared in June 1972 that Israel must find a way to thank President Nixon for his support, adding that he could not recall any past president who had committed himself to Israel to the extent that Nixon had. To some American Jews it appeared that Israel had quickly found a way, and that it was to bring pressure to bear on them to vote for Nixon. Despite Israeli Prime Minister Golda Meir's assurance to Senator Church that Israel was totally neutral on the American elections, accusations of Israeli pressure were bandied about in some Jewish circles in the United States and hotly denied in others. Mr Larry Phillips, President of the Phillips and Van Heusen Corporation, Chairman of the United Jewish Appeal in his industry and a millionaire backer of McGovern, publicly accused the Israeli leaders, through their 'vocal interference', of having torn the American Jewish community apart by speaking in Nixon's favour. 'I urge Israeli leaders MIX OUT!' he wrote and called on them to reconsider 'their policy of clandestine and subtle support for Nixon'.

Senator McGovern's strong suit from the point of view of many Jewish voters was his call for a revival of national values which, in the words of Rabbi Abraham Heschel of the Jewish Theological Seminary, 'echoed the demands of Israel's prophets'. By word and deed, he wrote, the Democratic candidate was committed to the idea that setting the moral tone of America was the most serious responsibility of a president. Regrettably the same could not be said of President Nixon. 'We must elect George McGovern to the Presidency of the United States because the needs of America and the values of our Jewish heritage demand it.'

President Nixon's strong suit was the fact that he was firmly in the saddle; his recent record of help to Israel; his policy on China and the Soviet Union; and his stand for discipline and order in social life. Towards the end of August, following complaints by the American Jewish Committee that the merit system was being destroyed, he ordered government departments to put an end to all quota systems in appointments and promotions. 'The way to end discrimination against some is not to begin discrimination against others,' he declared on 23 August in his acceptance speech at the Republican Convention. In that speech he referred only indirectly to Israel. To end the Vietnam war by imposing Communism on the people of Vietnam might be good politics, he asserted, but it would be disastrous to world peace; and 'in areas like the Mid-east, which are danger areas, small nations who rely on the friendship and support of the United States would be in deadly jeopardy'.

Although the President himself was reticent on Middle East issues, his campaign staff worked diligently to secure a larger share of the Jewish vote, especially in New York, where a shift to the Republican party would be most helpful to Nixon. During the summer months a big effort was launched in holiday camps to enlist 'foot soldiers'. It resulted in a growing band of volunteers, largely teachers and students, ready to drive cars, distribute literature and man department stores (eleven out of twenty storefronts in the city had what amounted to Jewish voter 'desks'). The 'literature' included a syndicated column pointing out that the Rogers Plan had been killed by the administration; a column from *Newsweek* by Stewart Alsop summarizing the President's commitments to Israel; and extracts from articles on McGovern's alleged opinions on such matters as quotas, permissiveness and other social issues. Campaign buttons proclaiming 'Nixon' in blue and white – the colours of Israel's flag – were widely distributed. In Los Angeles and Cleveland, as well as in New York, Nixon campaigners spread the word in storefront communiqués, bangle shops and meat markets, that the President understood better than the Democratic candidate the fears and hopes of the Jewish community; it was time for American Jews to break away from their traditional allegiance to the Democratic party.

The fight for the Jewish vote was marked, like the election campaign in general, by bizarre and tragic incidents. The issue of Soviet Jewry intruded somewhat grotesquely on to the scene. In August a Jewish Democratic Congressman and four colleagues made several unsuccessful attempts to call on Mr Dobrynin, the Soviet ambassador, with the object of giving him a million dollars to pay for exit visas recently imposed by the Soviet government on Jewish scientists and other holders of academic degrees wishing to emigrate to Israel (or so the measure was described in the American press – actually it applied to all Soviet citizens with academic qualifications wanting to emigrate to capitalist countries). The fees varied between £2,000 and £10,000 – sums far beyond the means of most Soviet citizens. This new Soviet action, which of course resulted in a storm of Zionist protests, was highly embarassing to the Republican campaigners; for the administration had let it be known that the whole question of the emigration of Soviet Jews to Israel had been discussed at the Moscow summit meeting. Mr Rogers hastened to assure Jewish leaders that the President had 'expressed concern' about the new move to the Soviet government. The administration was, above all, anxious that nothing be done to hold up the signature of the Soviet-American trade agreement, said to be worth $2,000 million by 1977, and the forthcoming strategic arms limitation talks. The Soviet Foreign Trade Minister was expected in Washington in the near future, presumably to sign the agreement, and a visit by the Soviet Communist party secretary, Leonid Brezhnev, was anticipated in the spring of 1973. To add to Republican embarrassment, New York Governor Nelson Rockefeller, on an election campaign visit to Israel, had reportedly announced that President Nixon had obtained in Moscow an agreement under which 35,000 Soviet Jews would be allowed to emigrate to Israel each year. This announcement, though later disowned by Rockefeller as a misquotation, was prominently reported in the American press and was assumed in most quarters to be the latest Republican bid for Jewish votes. Senator McGovern countered by declaring that if the Soviet Union were genuinely interested in improving relations with the United States, it would lift the restrictions imposed on Soviet Jews. 'I'm not willing to trade this country's historic commitment to human rights . . . just for commercial trade,' he told a meeting of Jewish leaders in New York on 21 September. Early in October the Senate weighed in by serving notice that it would block the passage of the trade agreement unless Moscow rescinded the exit visa fees. The Democratic candidate was one of seventy-one Senators – nearly three quarters of the Senate – who joined Senator Henry Jackson of Washington, a Democratic champion of Israel's territorial and other claims, in introducing an amendment in this sense. The Soviet government remained unmoved, contending that it had the right to levy fees to recover the cost of higher education and that measures to prevent the brain drain had been sanctioned by Unesco; and the Russian weekly, *Za Rubezhom* (*Abroad*), asked derisively, 'How can the presidential candidate of such a huge country, with all its tremendous problems, possibly have time to worry about emigration rules for Soviet citizens including Jews? Could this possibly be the key plank, actually little more than a splinter, on which the Democratic candidate expects to woo voters?'

Early in September a horrified world learned of the killing during the Munich Olympic Games of eleven Israeli athletes, five of their Black September Palestinian kidnappers and a West German policeman. President Nixon, Mr Rogers on behalf of the administration and Senator McGovern all voiced their sense of nausea and outrage over this terrible slaughter and the Democratic Majority Leader in the Senate called for the cancellation of the Olympic Games. The Israeli government urged the United States to recall its athletes from Munich. 'Israel's blood is not for the taking,' cried the Israeli Minister of the Interior, Yosef Burg. Reprisals in fact came two days later, in the form of an air attack on Syria and on Palestine refugee settlements in southern Lebanon. In Syria, where the Israelis had struck as far north as Hama and almost at the gates of Damascus, 200 dead and wounded were reported; in Lebanon, there were thirty-two deaths and twenty-seven wounded (seven children were among the dead and fourteen among the wounded); the Palestine commandos suffered 260 casualties, sixty of them fatal. The attack was followed by a search-and-destroy operation in Lebanon in mid-September, resulting in sixty deaths of Lebanese soldiers and the loss of sixty-one guerrillas. In France *Le Monde* had published an article on the day following the announcement of the Munich tragedy, pointing out that the terrible crime was the direct result of unredressed injustice done to the Palestinians, and this view had been echoed by several writers to the press in other countries, notably in Britain; but the sympathy of the civilized world and its leaders, after the Israeli reprisals had been reported, did not publicly go out to the families and friends of the dead Syrians, Lebanese and Palestinian refugees. Many of these new victims were stateless, without protection or acknowledged representation. As the writer of a letter to *The Times* put it, the lives of innocent human beings, including women and children, murdered by the Israelis were just as valuable, to them and to their families, as the lives of the Israeli athletes and their murder just as odious a crime – perhaps even more odious, since it was carried out by the armed forces of a sovereign state, not by a minority of irresponsible extremists. And a leading article in the *New York Times* of 18 October declared that it would be 'in Israel's own interest to seize the political as well as the military initiative, to start redressing the Palestinian grievance, which is one of the root problems of the Arab-Israel conflict'.

The immediate impact of the Munich tragedy on the American elections was a United States veto in the United Nations Security Council of a resolution introduced by Somalia, Guinea and Yugoslavia, calling for an end to all military activities in the Middle East and for the exercise of the greatest restraint. An emergency session of the council had been called by Syria and Lebanon to complain of Israel's attacks on their territory; the reason given for the veto by American representative George Bush was that the resolution contained no mention of the Munich killings. The veto marked a definite hardening of the American pro-Israel attitude, and was widely attributed to the coming elections. In June 1972 the United States had, in fact, merely abstained from a vote when the Security Council formally condemned Israel for attacks on Lebanon after the massacre at Lydda airport; this past voting record had been publicly criticized after the Munich disaster by Senator McGovern. For its part, the Council of the Arab League declared that the United States had, for domestic political reasons, supported Israeli aggression against Palestine refugee camps; while, in Jerusalem, the Foreign Minister, Eban, hailed the veto as of great international significance.

In the turmoil of the elections, what was the attitude of the tiny minority of Arab Americans, thought to number between half a million and a million and living for the most part in New York, Detroit and San Francisco? It is a community which has, incidentally, produced some well-known figures, among them the famous surgeon Dr Michael De Bakey, the great opera singer Rosalind Elias, and the consumers' champion Ralph Nader. The majority of Arab Americans pride themselves on their patriotism and identification with American interests, and until early September 1972 they were reported to be split on much the same lines as other ethnic groups: the older, more conservative and business-orientated individuals generally favouring Nixon and the younger people chiefly supporting McGovern. After the Munich tragedy and a call by McGovern, in a speech to the Southern Californian Board of Rabbis, for the punishment of Egypt and Lebanon because they harboured Palestinian terrorists, there was a greatly increased feeling of Arab solidarity and a strong tendency to close ranks. 'We are all disgusted with both the President and Senator McGovern for their strident support of Israel,' said one spokesman. The only attempt to redress the heavily pro-Israel position of Republicans and Democrats had, however, come earlier and from Governor Wallace, who had presented to the Democratic Convention in Miami a minority recommendation which would have committed the United States '. . . to strive in every way to merit and receive the friendship of all parties in the Arab-Israeli dispute and to earn the respect and good will of Israel and the Arab nations alike. . . '. His recommendation, needless to say, was rejected by the convention delegates.

The President's triumph on 8 November was over-whelming. He received 521 out of the 538 electoral votes and carried forty-nine of the fifty states, losing to Senator Mc-Govern only Massachusetts and the District of Columbia. Nixon's popular vote was 60.83 of the electorate, as compared to McGovern's 38 per cent. The Republican landslide was not paralleled in the Senate, where the Democrats increased their majority by two seats to fourteen, or in the House, where they lost thirteen seats but retained a majority of fifty. The first American of Arab descent to sit in the Senate, Democrat James Abouresk, won a vacancy in South Dakota left by a retiring Republican Senator. Experts estimated that President Nixon had received three times as many Jewish votes as in 1968 and that his percentage of such votes in predominantly Jewish districts was between 40 and 50 per cent. 'One sure outcome of the election campaign,' predicted Jacob Stein, Chairman of the Conference of Presidents of Major American Jewish Organizations, 'is that the Democrats will never take the Jewish vote for granted again.' Arab public opinion in the Middle East was, generally speaking, unmoved by the result, having all along taken the view that, whoever won the election, there would be no change in United States policy on Arab-Israel affairs. But *Al Moharrer*, often believed to voice the opinions of the Palestine Liberation Organization, called for the mobilization of all Arab nationalist energies to block any new United States initiative that disregarded Palestinian aspirations.

10. CONCLUSIONS

It is twenty-five years since the Arabs of Palestine lost their country. For the great majority of Americans, as for Mrs Meir, the Prime Minister of Israel, there is no such thing as a Palestinian people. On the world scene, their case has gone largely by default. Since 1947 they have been represented at the annual sessions of the United Nations General Assembly, but only on sufferance, as a politically anonymous, inferior group outside the family of nations. At the insistence of the delegates of the Arab states, the political kernel of the Arab-Israel conflict has, it is true, been debated year after year in New York – but under the nominal heading of assistance to refugees. Arab speakers have pleaded the Palestinian case, but there has been little echo of their eloquence in the world outside and it has had perceptibly no impact on the American consciousness. Until very recently, if Americans ever thought of the Palestine Arabs, it was as a faceless mass of refugees living in flimsy tents, as no doubt they were accustomed to do and as they at any rate deserved to live.

The United States and the Soviet Union see the Arab-Israel conflict as a matter to be resolved through inter-governmental negotiation: the Palestinians are not a national party to the dispute. For the two Arab states most directly concerned, Egypt and Jordan, Israel's withdrawal from their territories is the crucial issue. Practically nothing is heard of the heart of the matter: the denial of the Palestinian people's right to their homeland. It is not surprising that no progress towards a settlement has been made.

Had the Palestine Arabs in 1947 not been weak, divided among themselves, diplomatically inexperienced and so deeply convinced of the injustice of the UNSCOP partition proposals that they believed the partition plan could not possibly be sanctioned by the world organization, it is just conceivable that the proposed Arab state might have come into being in a legal, orderly fashion in 1948 and that an 'Arab' section of Palestine would have achieved equal dignity, status, rights and responsibilities with other United Nations members. But the Palestine Arabs did not manage to achieve statehood in 1948 and have suffered from the loss of it ever since.

The concept of a 'special relationship' between the United States and Israel was first put into words by President Kennedy: but it began in October 1948, when President Truman, deeply influenced by Zionist friends, not oblivious of the presidential election then pending, but sincerely convinced that the Zionist state was a fine and just achievement, declared that America was 'pledged to a state of Israel large enough, free enough and strong enough to make its people self-supporting and secure'. Since that day the American commitment has snowballed with every passing year. Even Eisenhower, the only president who has succeeded in making the Government of Israel change course at a time of crisis, felt that the United States had obligations to Israel and that these must be kept. Kennedy gave Eshkol in the autumn of 1963 a written assurance of a *de facto* guarantee of Israel's territorial integrity. Johnson had to walk a tightrope in 1967 between his commitment to stand four-square behind Israel and the paramount need, if a Third World War was to be averted, to ensure non-intervention by both America and

Russia. Nixon, who withheld for two years, despite terrific congressional pressure, the military aid the Zionists were desperately seeking, nevertheless surpassed all his predecessors in his massive support of Israel once the reasons for his decision to defer aid had disappeared. All American politicans recognize and take into consideration the 'Jewish interest' factor in domestic politics. Middle East experts in government service, no matter how clearly they understand the Arab viewpoint, assume that the commitment to Israel is an accepted fact with which the United States has to live.

What has this relationship meant in practical terms? As an American diplomat pointed out in a letter to *The Times* in early 1971, it has gone far beyond links that the United States once had with Great Britain. In December 1970, the Senate killed an amendment to the Defence Appropriations Bill which would have forbidden the United States to send troops to Israel without congressional permission. In violation of the regulations of the United States Internal Revenue Service, of the equal protection clauses of the American consititution and of certain provisions of the Civil Rights Act of 1963, contributions from Americans to the United Jewish Appeal and the United Israel Appeal are treated as tax exempt. According to a recent interpretation by the Supreme Court, Americans are allowed to vote in Israeli elections and serve in Israel's armed forces and civil service without losing their American citizenship. During the first twenty years of Israel's existence, economic aid from the U.S. government and dollar transfers from private sources amounted to $36,000 million, or $1,400 *per capita* (as compared with an average of $35 *per capita* given to thirteen neighbouring countries). Since 1967, the United States has given Israel aircraft, missiles and electronic systems of a more advanced and sophisticated type than those she has made available to her NATO and SEATO allies. Israel has been provided with the most up-to-date information on the use of nuclear weapons and, alone among over a hundred nations, was not subject to American pressure to adhere to the Nuclear Non-Proliferation Treaty; for years nuclear reactors in Israel have reportedly been producing enough plutonium for ten 25-kiloton bombs a year. The Israeli air strikes that opened the war on 5 June 1967 were partly based on intelligence provided by American sources. Most extraordinary of all, appointments to State Department senior posts concerned with Middle East policy have traditionally been subject to prior approval by the American Zionist leadership. Finally Israel, alone among America's friends and allies, seems to be practically immune from public blame or even criticism.

The paradox of all this is that, while it is clear that such a relationship is a lifeline for Israel and a disaster for the Palestine Arabs, it is difficult to understand why it should be supposed to advance America's own national interests. The Arab Middle East would seem to be important to the United States, first, because it is rich in oil; secondly, because, situated at the meeting point of three continents, it provides transportation routes in which America has both military and civilian interests; thirdly, because America's goal was first, to prevent, and now is to limit Soviet power and influence in the region and in the Eastern Mediterranean generally. A policy of unwavering support for Israel sticks up like a sore thumb in the midst of a general Middle East policy based on these interests. Three quarters of the world's known petroleum reserves are in the Arab Middle East: two years ago only 3 per cent of America's domestic needs came from this source. Experts have predicted that, by 1980, the United States will perforce be obliged to import more than half its domestic needs and that one third will have to come from the Middle East. Early in January 1973, Rogers Morton, Secretary of the Interior, told a congressional committee that the United States was 'on the very brink of real hardcore supply shortage which could develop over the next two or three years if we don't do anything about it'. On 14 January the administration decided that the United States would have to become dependent upon Arab countries for its energy supplies. In the circumstances, it is not easy to see how America will be able to continue for long a Middle East policy completely at loggerheads with Arab aspirations.

In the field of transportation, the refusal of Syria and Lebanon to allow the Sixth Fleet to use their port facilities and the closure by Libya of the Wheelus Air Force base are indications of the extent to which America's pro-Israel stand has made her vulnerable. And far from preventing Soviet penetration into the area, the United States has played into Russia's hands. As far back as 1950, the Soviet Union saw that American policy on Palestine would alienate the Arabs and encourage them to turn to the Eastern bloc for support. When in 1955 the Baghdad Pact was announced and immediately interpreted by Nasser as hostile to his aims, the direct consequence was the Czech arms deal, as a result of which the Soviet Union obtained its first foothold in the region. America's brusque withdrawal from support of the Aswan Dam led in quick succession to the nationalization of the Suez Canal, the Suez War and the open championship of Egypt by Russia. The net result of the Eisenhower Doctrine in 1957 was further to enhance Soviet prestige in the region and to prompt Syria to turn to Russia for economic and military aid. In short, American Middle East policy has not only been unjust and unco-ordinated, it has also been self-defeating.

In a pluralistic, democratic society like that of the United States, minority groups are expected to express their views and to endeavour to bring some influence to bear on public policy. After the Second World War, Polish Americans urged hostility to the Communist government in Warsaw; American Catholics campaigned vigorously for intervention on Franco's side in the Spanish Civil War; Dutch Americans had pressed for United States involvement in the Boer War. But that a group representing just under 3 per cent of the total population of the United States should wield such inordinate political power and use it for purposes felt by many to be frequently harmful to the national interest, is an extraordinary phenomenon. 'The only ally we have is the Jewish people,' wrote Ben Gurion in 1957. The over six million American Jews, wealthy and influential out of proportion to their numbers, are the largest group of Jews in the world (the three million Soviet Jews ranking second), and their emotional ties with Israel and sense of responsibility for her well-being are very strong. They themselves see no conflict of interest between Israel and the United States. Without the power they were able to exert, the State of Israel could not have been established in 1948, nor would the unique United States–Israel relationship have been consolidated. Over the years, the leaders of American Zionist organizations have pertinaceously made their views known to the White House and to the Congress, urging the giving of arms to Israel, withholding of arms and aid from the Arabs, a guarantee of Israel's security, less financial assistance for Arab refugees, a softer line on Israel's retaliatory measures, free passage of Israeli shipping through the Suez Canal, the elimination of the threat of sanctions against Israel. Not all of these moves were successful, but the pressure has been maintained unremittingly, often backed up by public demonstrations and protest meetings and always supported by the power American Zionists can exert on the press and helped by the high proportion of Zionist sympathizers in the information media and by the admiration for Israel felt by many liberal and intellectual Americans.

No corresponding Arab pressure-group emerged. The Arabs themselves had neither the wealth nor the expertise to secure a fair hearing for the Palestinian case. Despite the courageous efforts of recently formed groups aiming at increasing American understanding of the Arab viewpoint, the Palestinian Arabs remain shadowy figures and their case is, for the most part, not only misunderstood but totally ignored.

The outlook for Arab–Israel peace seems at first sight to be as far off as it ever was. All attempts to reach a settlement in the wake of the 1967 war have foundered on the rock of Israel's insistence that her security cannot be guaranteed unless she retains almost all the territories she occupied during that war. The United Nations is powerless in the face of Israel's defiance, because of the near certainty of a United States veto on any form of sanctions against the Zionist state. Each successive Israeli victory has strengthened the Arab refusal to accept her existence: they have experienced only too bitterly the truth of Bertrand Russell's dictum that every Israeli expansionist move is also an experiment to discover how much more aggression the world will tolerate.

But certain movements are stirring that may bring about a more hopeful situation in the not too distant future. The Palestine resistance movement has become the most dynamic element in the Arab Middle East. It has tried to topple the ruling establishment in Jordan, played a part in overthrowing the monarchy in Libya, been involved in an unsuccessful *coup* in Saudi Arabia. Its attack on an El-Al plane resulted in Israel's raid on Beirut Airport in December 1968: which in turn led to the fall of the Lebanese government. Since the Israeli government regards the Arab countries which harbour the Palestine guerrillas as responsible for their attacks, the resistance movement can bring pressure on Arab governments for more militant action. Despite its integral dissensions, despite the profound shock to world public opinion caused by Palestinian terrorist outrages, the Arabs of Palestine have at last brought about a situation where the word 'Palestinian' is no longer synonymous with 'refugee'. Even an American Middle East expert has suggested that it would be in the interests of all parties to the dispute, and of the United States itself, if the Palestinians had a recognized voice in negotiations for a settlement.

The most positive and encouraging development is, however, the growing recognition in Israel itself, and not only among the young and the 'New Left', that the Palestine Arabs were wronged when the Zionist state was created. The Israeli labour leader, Arye Elav, a key member of Mrs Meir's political family and a former adviser and close friend of Levi Eshkol, has been travelling the country declaring that Israel's duty and best interests lie in taking steps to redress the grievances of the Palestinians and has demanded that Israel announce her readiness to recognize a Palestine Arab state in most areas of the West Bank and the Gaza Strip (plus East Jordan). In a book published in August 1972 and subtitled 'An evaluation of the possibilities open to Israel', Elav calls on the Government of Israel to come to terms with the

Palestine Arabs and recognize their historical rights, adding that an Israeli-Egyptian peace would not solve the problem, the core of which is formed by the Palestinians. And the crisis of conscience showed itself in the storm of protest which arose in Israel in the summer of 1972 among both Jews and Arabs over the government's refusal to allow Arab villagers living in Israel to return to the site of their former homes, bulldozed twenty-four years ago. Meanwhile, Dr Nahum Goldmann, President of the World Jewish Congress, pointing out that Israel had already antagonized large parts of the progressive world, has called for the 'neutralization' of Israel and her survival as a spiritual centre of Jewish civilization.

On the American front, too, there are some hopeful signs. Those Arab states which are rich in oil can expect, in the light of America's new and growing dependence on Arab oil, to be able to exert increased leverage on United States policy. On the eve of the 1972 election, President Nixon gave an interview (not published until after the results had been announced) in which he stressed that the explosive Middle East situation would have very high priority during his second administration. It is not impossible that, during Nixon's second term, steps as dramatic and revolutionary as his visit to Peking and the détente with Moscow will be taken in a new effort to bring about a Middle East settlement. Whether or not this happens, it is difficult to imagine that even the stubborn Arab–Israel conflict could long survive as a solitary centre of tension in an atmosphere of long-term Russian-American détente.

The 'special relationship' between the United States and Israel has led to seemingly indefinite injustice to the Palestine Arabs; but the relationship could still, if wisely used by the major partner, open the door to an Arab–Israel settlement and to some sort of rough justice – for at this late stage it could not be more – for the Palestinians. America still holds the key. In the long term, peace in the Middle East – and for that matter the survival of Israel – will depend on the relations Israel herself is ultimately able to build with the Arab world.

SELECTED
BIBLIOGRAPHY

Acheson, Dean, *Power and Diplomacy*, Harvard University Press, Cambridge, Mass., 1958

Acheson, Dean, *Present at the Creation, My Years in the State Department*, Hamish Hamilton, London, 1970

Azcarate, Pablo de, *Mission in Palestine, 1948–1952*, the Middle East Institute, Washington, 1966

Bernadotte, Count Folke, *To Jerusalem*, Hodder and Stoughton, London, 1951

Brecher, Michael, *The Foreign Policy System of Israel*, Oxford University Press, London, 1972

Burns, Lieutenant-General E. L. M., *Between Arab and Israeli*, Harrap, London, 1962

Davis, John H., *The Evasive Peace, A Study of the Zionist/Arab Problem*, John Murray, London, 1968

Eden, Sir Anthony, *Full Circle*, Cassell, London, 1960

Eisenhower, Dwight D., *The White House Years, Waging Peace, 1956–1961*, Heinemann, London, 1966

Elath, Eliahu, *Israel and Elath*, Weidenfeld and Nicolson, London, 1966 (for the Jewish Historical Society)

187

Evans, Rowland Jr. and Robert D. Novak, *Nixon in the White House*, Random House, New York, 1972

Finer, Herman, *Dulles over Suez*, Heinemann, London, 1964

Furlonge, Sir Geoffrey, *Palestine Is My Country, The Story of Musa Alami*, John Murray, London, 1969

Forrestal, James, *The Forrestal Diaries, The Inner History of the Cold War* (ed. Walter Millis), Cassell, London, 1952

Glubb, Sir John Bagot, *Peace in the Holy Land, an Historical Analysis of the Political Problem*, Hodder and Stoughton, London, 1971

Goldmann, Nahum, *Memories*, Weidenfeld and Nicolson, London, 1970

Heikal, Mohamed Hassanein, *The Cairo Documents*, New English Library, London, 1972

Horowitz, David, *State in the Making*, Knopf, New York, 1953

Howard, H. N., *The King-Crane Commission: An American Inquiry in the Middle East*, Khayats, Beirut, 1963

Hull, Cordell, *The Memoirs of Cordell Hull*, Volume II, Hodder and Stoughton, London, 1948

Hurewitz, J. C., *The Struggle for Palestine*, W. W. Norton, New York, 1950

Jansen, Michael E., *The United States and the Palestinian People*, The Institute for Palestine Studies, Beirut, 1970

Jiryis, Sabri, *The Arabs in Israel, 1948–1966*, The Institute for Palestine Studies, Beirut, 1968

Johnson, Lyndon Baines, *The Vantage Point: Perspectives of the Presidency, 1963–1969*, Weidenfeld and Nicolson, London, 1972

Kirk, George E., *The Middle East in the War, 1939–1946, Survey of International Affairs*, Royal Institute of International Affairs, Oxford University Press, London, 1952

Kirk, George E., *The Middle East 1945–1950, Survey of International Affairs*, Royal Institute of International Affairs, Oxford University Press, London, 1954

Laquer, Walter, *The Soviet Union and the Middle East*, Routledge and Kegan Paul, London, 1959

Laquer, Walter, *The Road to War 1967: The Origin of the Arab-Israel Conflict*, Weidenfeld and Nicolson, London, 1968

Lie, Trygve, *In the Cause of Peace: Seven Years with the United Nations*, Macmillan, New York, 1954

Lilienthal, Alfred M., *What Price Israel?*, Henry Regnery, Chicago, 1953

Love, Kennett, *Suez: The Twice-Fought War*, Longmans Green, London, 1970

McDonald, James G., *My Mission in Israel, 1948–1951*, Gollancz, London, 1951

Nes, David G., 'America's Very Special Relationship with Israel', *Middle East International,* April 1971

Nes, David G., 'Israel and the American Election', *Middle East International*, October 1972

Pearlman, Moshe, *Ben Gurion Looks Back in Talks with Moshe Pearlman*, Weidenfeld and Nicolson, London, 1965

Rodinson, Maxime, *Israel and the Arabs*, Penguin Books, Harmondsworth, 1968

Rondot, Pierre, *The Changing Patterns of the Middle East*, Chatto and Windus, London, 1961

Roosevelt, Kermit, 'The Partition of Palestine: A Lesson in Pressure Politics', *Middle East Journal,* January 1948

Safran, Nadav, *The United States and Israel*, Oxford University Press, London, 1963

Stevens, Richard P., *American Zionism and U.S. Foreign Policy, 1942–1947*, Pageant Press, New York, 1962

Sykes, Christopher, *Cross Roads to Israel*, Collins, London, 1965

Truman, Harry S., *The Memoirs of Harry S. Truman*, Volume II: *Years of Trial and Hope, 1946–1953*, Hodder and Stoughton, London, 1956

Turki, Fawaz, *The Disinherited: Journal of a Palestinian Exile*, Monthly Review Press, New York, 1972

Williams, Francis, *A Prime Minister Remembers: War and Post-war Memoirs of Lord Attlee*, Heinemann, London, 1961

Yost, Charles, 'The Arab-Israel War, How It Began', *Foreign Affairs*, January 1968

INDEX

192